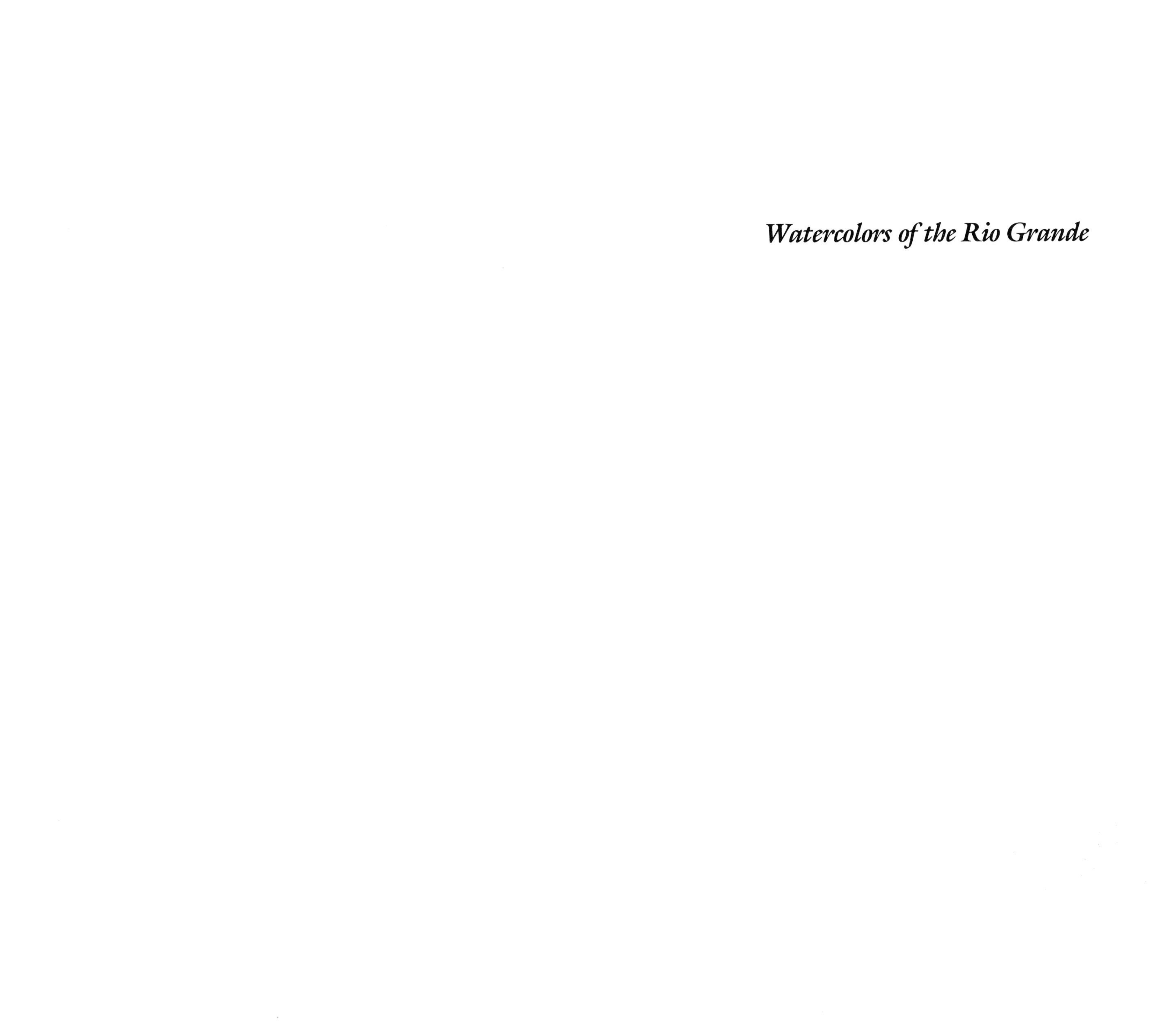

Watercolors of the Rio Grande

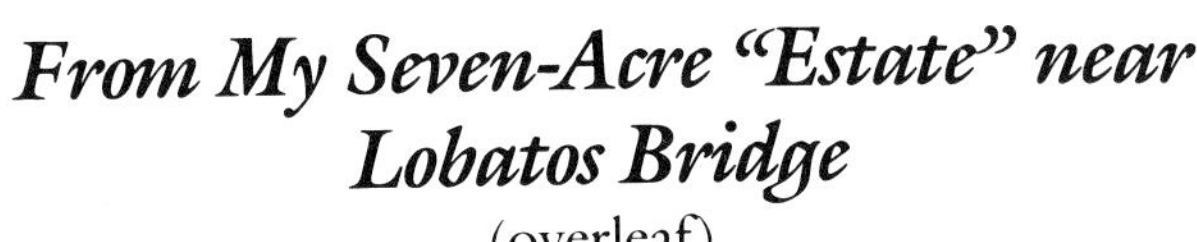

From My Seven-Acre "Estate" near Lobatos Bridge

(overleaf)

This was my first painting of the Rio Grande, looking north toward Mount Blanca from my seven acres near Lobatos Bridge. The gorge starts here, and the canyon walls rise about twenty feet above the water. Six miles south, at the Colorado–New Mexico border, the cliffs tower about two hundred feet into the sky. I saw many petroglyphs in this area, indicating that at one time many more people lived in this vicinity than they do today. The nearest town is Antonito, fifteen miles due west on a dirt road.

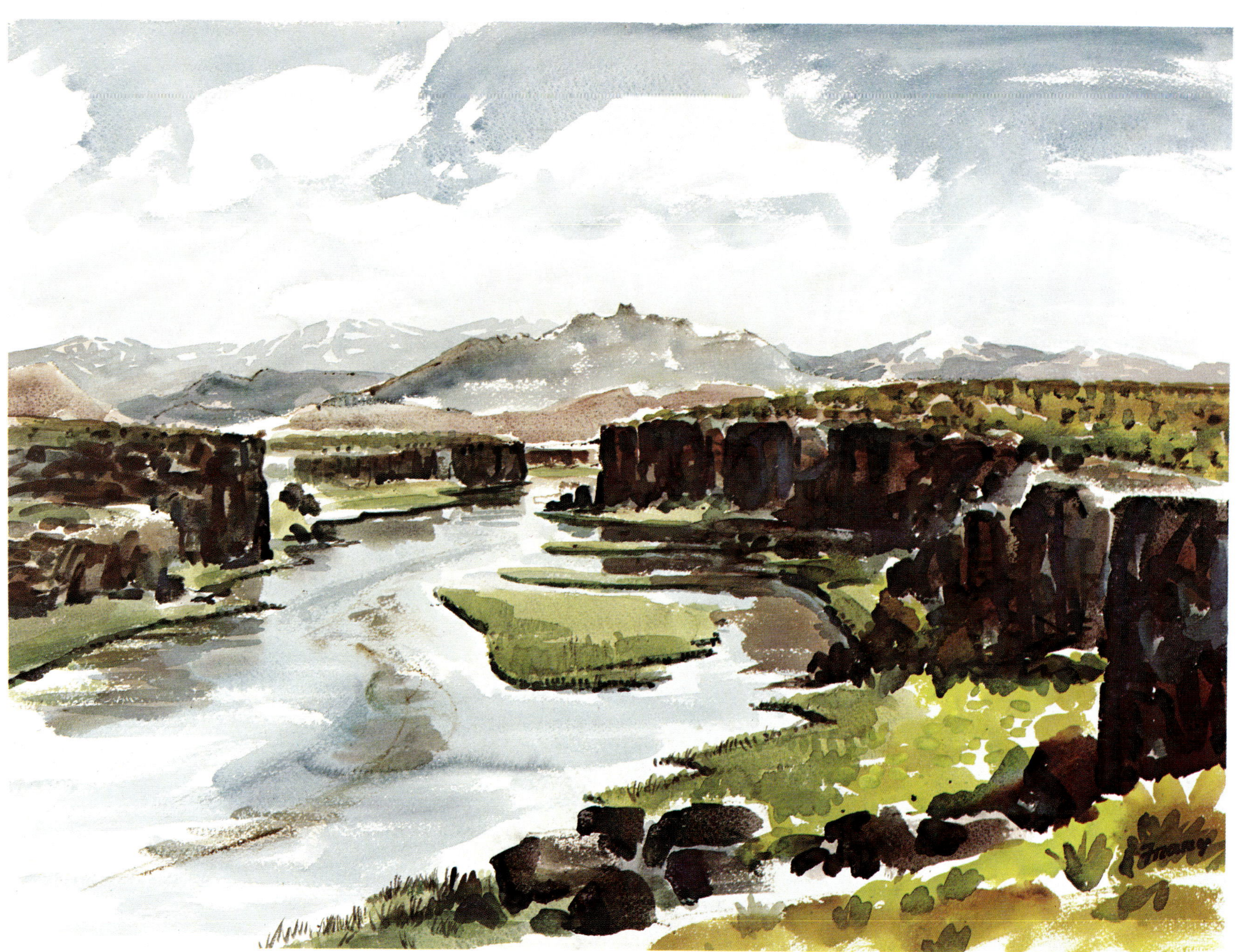

Watercolors of the Rio Grande

By MICHAEL FRARY

TEXAS A&M UNIVERSITY PRESS *College Station*

Library of Congress Cataloging in Publication Data

Frary, Michael, 1918–
Watercolors of the Rio Grande.

1. Frary, Michael, 1918– 2. Rio Grande in art.
I. Title.
ND1839.F69A4 1984 759.13 84-40128
ISBN 0-89096-207-3

Manufactured in the United States of America
FIRST EDITION

To the memory of Dale H. Dorn, whose interest and enthusiasm helped make the publication of this book a reality

Contents

Preface

I decided to produce a series of paintings pertaining to the Rio Grande because to me it had an unusual sense of mystery and romance, and I wanted to find out more about it. After reading the definitive book on the river's history, Paul Horgan's *Great River: The Rio Grande in North American History* (New York: Rinehart & Co., 1954), I became convinced that this river is extremely important historically. As to size, it is exceeded in length only by the Mississippi-Missouri system in North America. It gives its all to irrigate millions of acres of farmland. I discovered, however, that the river's unique element is its diversity: it has raging torrents as well as dry riverbeds, clear trout streams and stagnant marshes, meandering tropical areas and spectacular gorges.

About fifteen years ago, my wife and I bought seven acres along the river at the beginning of the Rio Grande Gorge. I began this series of paintings at that time. Since then, I have camped and painted on its banks from the headwaters to the mouth. I have swum and canoed in it and have explored not only its well-known areas but also those parts that are almost inaccessible. It is my favorite river. Some of my fascination with and awe of the Rio Grande is, I hope, expressed in these watercolor paintings.

Many of these watercolors were done on the spot, while sitting on the ground or in my mobile "studio," a Volkswagen bus. The paintings are in the transparent watercolor medium (no white paint used), and all are on French "Arches" watercolor paper. I used both 140 lb. and 300 lb. cold-pressed, Imperial size (22″ x 30″) sheets.

It has been both an exciting challenge and an educational experience to produce these paintings. As an artist, it is extremely gratifying to see my work reproduced in book form. An endeavor of this magnitude, however, could not have been undertaken without the help of many. First, I want to extend my appreciation to my wife, Peggy, without whose constant assistance and patience my Rio Grande project could never have reached fulfillment. My thanks to the art department of the University of Texas at Austin for a grant that enabled me to travel and paint the river several more times than would otherwise have been possible. I am grateful to Texas A&M University Press for their continuing policy of producing high-quality art books. Also, my thanks to the many people who gave me their expertise on different aspects of the river. Finally, I extend my deep appreciation to Betty Coates Maddux, the Dale Dorn family, and the Richardson B. Gill family, without whose generous support this book would not have been published. I hope that their confidence in my work will in a small way be rewarded in the knowledge that the magnificent and awesome beauty of the Rio Grande, one of America's wonders, will unfold before the readers of this book.

It seemed to me appropriate to take the advice of a leader of one of my canoe trips who said, in regard to running a river, you should usually "go with the flow." So we begin the long journey at Stony Pass, on the backbone of the United States, and "go with the flow" to Boca Chica ("little mouth"), on the Gulf of Mexico.

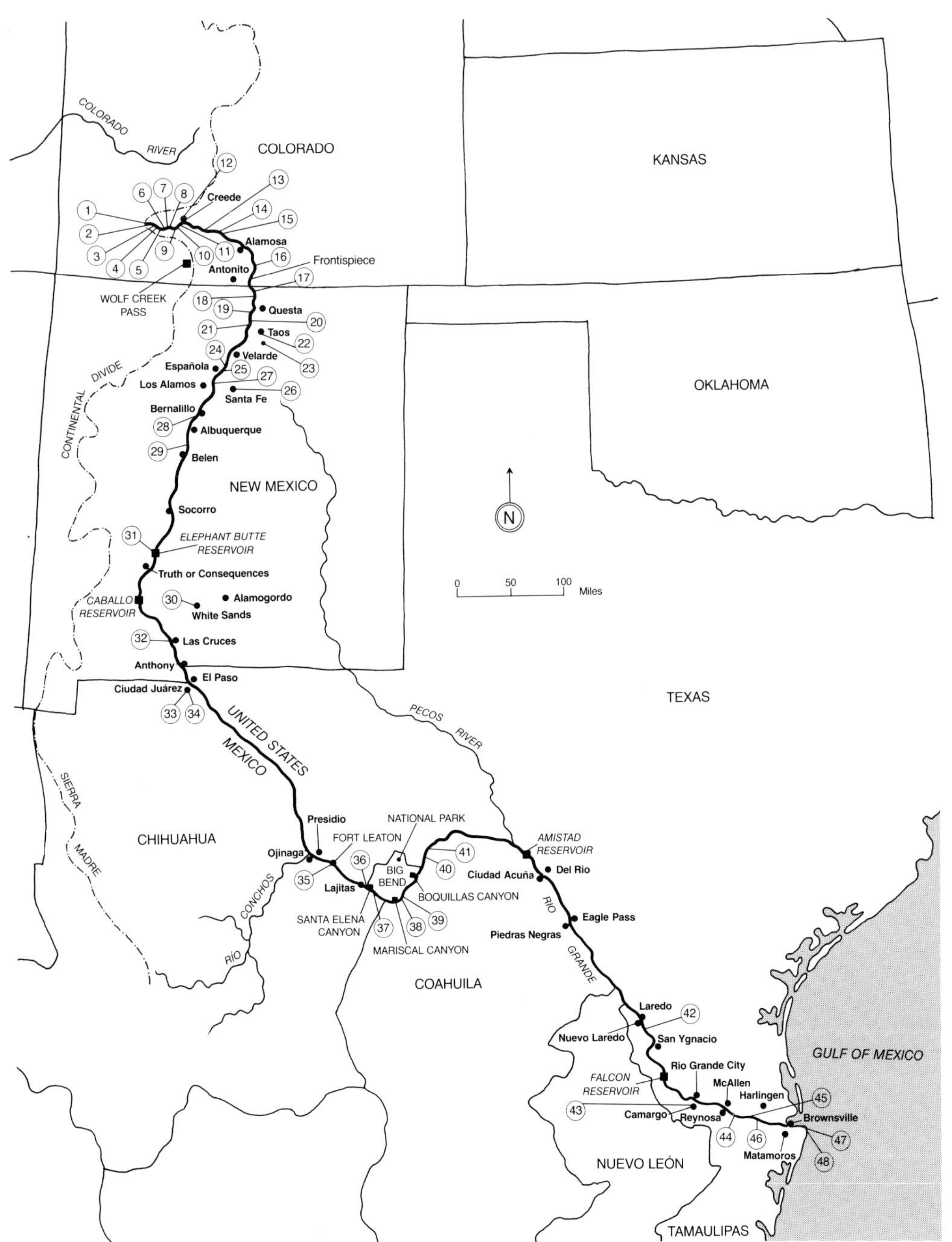

The course of the Rio Grande as it winds southward from Creede, Colorado, to the Gulf of Mexico. The numbers on the map refer to the sequence of paintings in the book. Each number pinpoints the location where the corresponding watercolor was painted.

Part One: The Colorado Rio Grande

The Colorado Rio Grande

I had a growing sense of anticipation and suspense as I drove up past Wagon Wheel Gap deep in the mountains of Colorado. I was headed for the source of the Rio Grande for the first time. The temperature was dropping, and the air seemed to be charged with electricity from the violent storm ahead in the majestic San Juan Mountains. The clouds partially obscured some of the massive, silent peaks. I felt that I was going up into a secret world—into the elemental forces of nature.

I camped that night at Lost Trail Creek, which is as far as a two-wheel-drive vehicle can go. The next morning I went back to a small guest ranch and engaged a jeep and driver to take me to the top of Stony Pass. The last fifteen miles caused me a little anxiety. From the passenger's seat, I leaned out and looked almost straight down about one thousand feet. The driver told me that the "road" was built by Chinese coolies in 1889 after rich silver strikes at Silverton to the west and at Creede to the east. Because the road was too rough for wagons, heavy mining equipment was hauled from Creede to Silverton on wooden sleds, jerked forward foot by foot by mules. I am positive there has been no effort to improve the road since then.

From the top of the pass on the Continental Divide looking east, I could see a wide valley surrounded on both sides by peaks 13,000 to 14,000 feet high. Close to Stony Pass are Sunlight, Windom, Wilson, Sunshine, Handies, Red Cloud, and Uncompahgre peaks, and Mounts Eolus, Sneffels, and Wilson, all over 14,000 feet in elevation. On this late July day, the irregular enclosure of the upper valley was gray-green, spotted with the white of snowbanks that refused to melt. The pass at over 12,500 feet is far above the timberline, and the vegetation consists of a profusion of attractive wild flowers, alpine grasses, sedges, lichens, and other hardy plants associated with the Arctic-Alpine life zone. These grasses and other small plants give the slopes their green tint in summer.

The animals I saw were the tailless, rabbitlike pikas, sometimes called "calling hares" because of their shrill whistle. I also saw large (up to 30 inches long) marmots, a type of woodchuck. Marmots are occasionally dubbed "whistle pigs" because of their sharp, high-pitched whistling call. It seems that there are two schools of thought as to whether the pikas or the marmots make the whistle. Perhaps both do. In any case, these animals appeared and disappeared magically among the sharp, cubelike rocks and boulders. I spotted a herd of elk jumping and rolling in a distant snowbank, trying, the driver said, to rid themselves of the tenacious high-altitude flies. The most interesting bird I saw was a water pipit that walked upstream, sometimes underwater. There are other birds here, including the golden eagle, rosy finch, and horned lark. It is surprising how many animals and plants have adapted to and can survive in this lonely, harsh land.

After walking around for a while, getting the feel of the place, I sat down on the boggy slope and began painting a snowbank designated by an official-looking sign as the "headwaters of the Rio Grande." I was immediately impressed by the dark blue of the sky against the white snowbank. The crystal-clear air made the sunlight sparkle like diamonds on the snow.

After I had worked for ten or fifteen minutes, I suddenly realized that the canvas I was sitting on had several inches of ice water on it. The top of the permafrost was melting, as well as the snowbank. Water was everywhere, and it was all flowing into a foot-wide gully that was to become the Great River. As I was painting on this "hot" day, I tried to imagine what this area would be like in the winter. There would be deep compacted snow, temperatures of sixty degrees below zero, and winds of one hundred miles per hour. It would be difficult to paint on the spot under those conditions. I did, however, paint in fifteen-degree weather at lower altitudes. The washes froze and the ice crystals evaporated, leaving very interesting textures and icy designs. I was told that a record was set in the winter of 1979–80 at Wolf Creek Pass (considerably lower than Stony Pass), when some 842 inches of snow, or seventy feet, were measured. One inch of water is usually the result of one foot of snowmelt in the Rocky Mountains.

After that winter, over a billion and a half tons of water came thundering down the tributaries into the Rio Grande. Before the river was checked by reservoirs, it must indeed have been a wild river, or Río Bravo, as the Spanish called it, and the Mexicans still do. In the spring and summer the gullies and rills become rivers, and Pole Creek, Bear Creek, Lost Trail Creek, and Ute Creek become roaring cataracts with many spectacular waterfalls. In late summer the creeks are tumbling streams, and in winter everything is silent and frozen.

The water is controlled by reservoirs and lakes on many of the tributaries, but the first and major control of the upper valley water is the Rio Grande Reservoir. The earthen dam blocks a narrow canyon and was built about seventy years ago by a group of farmers in the San Luis Valley. The lake thus formed varies greatly in size but may be five to seven miles long and one-half mile wide. The shoreline rocks are covered with silvery green lichen. In the summer, the plants next to the lake take on a low-intensity color scheme of silvery raw umber, yellow ocher, and burnt sienna, with an occasional touch of purple.

As I was painting the reservoir from the top of the dam, the daily afternoon summer storm came up. It turned cold. As I started to scratch out whitecaps on my painting it began to rain and hail, so I had to get under cover.

From the dam downstream for fifty miles, the river is an ideal trout stream—clean, clear, and cold with many rainbow trout and many fishermen. On the way down I could see the towering mountains to the north, which comprise the La Garita Wilderness, and the Weminuche Wilderness farther south. Forty miles from the top of the pass the dirt road becomes paved, and the valley broadens into the upper meadows, where, for the first time, I saw water used to irrigate a few hundred acres of hay fields. The river spreads out and becomes marshlike with reeds, waterfowl, and big mosquitoes. I saw many beaver dams along the way. Beavers played an important role in this area's history. At one time beaver hats were popular in the large cities, and, as a result, there were many beaver trappers. Many of these rugged mountain men later became scouts and led expeditions to the West.

The river drops quickly from the Arctic-Alpine zone through the Hudsonian zone, with its handsome one-hundred-twenty-foot Englemann spruce and its limber pines. At about ten thousand feet in elevation, the top limits of the Canadian life zone, the aspen make a tapestry design with the darker lodgepole pines, Douglas firs, and ponderosa pines. Aspen are interesting. They grow from the spreading roots of other aspen, so they tend to grow in clumps. Their trunks are white, and in spring and summer the leaves are a light jade green. The color of the leaves gradually turns, and in October they are a brilliant golden yellow. The leaves flutter in the slightest breeze, hence the name "quaking aspen." The patchwork-quilt design of the trees follows the river down past the massive Bristol Head Mountain, and then, surprisingly, the river runs northeast to the picturesque town of Creede, fifty-five miles downstream from the headwaters.

Nicholas Creede struck silver on Willows Creek in 1889 and started the last of the big silver booms. Creede, in 1892, had more than ten thousand inhabitants and at least one hundred hotels. It was a wild and rowdy boom town, with Bat Masterson trying to keep some law and order. Cigar-smoking Poker Alice, with her friends Calamity Jane and Slanting Annie, were some of the popular "soiled doves." Some of the ore from the Amethyst Mine was so rich it yielded five thousand dollars a ton.

Creede is still a mining town. The large Emperius Mine's gross profits exceeded $30 million in thirty-five years of operation. Creede suffered several devastating fires and floods but was rebuilt, and today it is popular with tourists, sportsmen, and miners. (I haven't heard of any contemporary Slanting Annies.) This picturesque mountain town has a population of about three hundred fifty. The Denver and Rio Grande Railway downstream becomes part of the landscape. Ten miles downriver, past McKinney Gulch ski lift, there is a fine depot at Wagon Wheel Gap. This is one of my favorite spots. The valley narrows, and the river seems to pick up speed through the gap. A resident told me that in the winter of 1979 it was fifty-eight degrees below zero, and the snow piled up to the telephone lines.

The next village downstream is at the confluence of the Rio Grande and the South Fork River, which flows from the Wolf Creek area. At the town of South Fork, the river leaves the Rio Grande National Forest. Large pines are replaced by stubby piñon pines, oaks, and juniper, and cottonwoods begin to line the banks of the river. Mountains dwindle to low rolling hills. Vegetation decreases, and herds of sheep appear. At Del Norte, a town of about two thousand, the treeless hills end with a bare, round outcropping called Elephant Rock. Across the fifty miles due east rise the formidable peaks of Blanca, Lindsey, and Little Bear, all over fourteen thousand feet in elevation. These peaks are in the Sangre de Cristo range, which forms the eastern barrier to the Rio Grande.

After traveling some 135 miles from its source, the Rio Grande finally makes a large, sweeping arc and assumes its destined direction, due south, which it will follow until it reaches the Mexican border. The river passes through the San Luis Valley, a large, flat desert seventy-five hundred feet high, surrounded by mountains. As it flows into the valley, the Rio Grande is diverted into a series of canals and many laterals, ditches, and drains, which irrigate about 700,000 acres. The big Del Norte ditch alone diverts over fifteen hundred cubic feet of water per second. The excess water is collected and returned to the river in drains and is used over and over again. This has resulted in a fertile valley with a variety of crops extending many miles from the riverbed.

The towns of Del Norte, Monte Vista, and Alamosa are

thriving business communities with their potatoes, lettuce, and barley processing plants. I was impressed with the cleanliness of these towns and by the many purple-leafed crab apple trees lining the streets. Because of the allocation of water to the north, most of the valley south of here remains a semiarid, cool, high-altitude desert. It is sagebrush country with no trees, where only chamisa, rabbit sage, grama grass, and chico bush grow. I was told by the leader of one of my canoe trips that any small, unknown bush is called "chico bush."

The first permanent settlement in this area (actually in all of Colorado) was founded by Spanish pioneers. They came northward from Taos in the early 1800s and settled in the southeast San Luis Valley.

In the valley lived hostile, nomadic Indians: the Comanches from the east, the Sioux and Cheyenne from the north, and the Utes and Apaches from this area and the west. As a defense against attack, early white settlers built homes around plazas with no windows in their exterior walls. After much fighting between the Indians and the settlers, the United States finally gave the Utes the title to a perpetual reservation in the San Juan Mountains in 1868 and took over the valley. But after gold and silver were discovered in the mountains, the Utes were evicted from this "perpetual reservation" in their beloved mountains and forced to move to an overgrazed patch of desert in southwestern Colorado. In this way the Indians were compelled to give up their heritage in the San Luis Valley. It remained for the Pueblo Indians in the Española Valley to the south to survive the encroachment of "civilization" and to provide the rich historical heritage of the Indian-Spanish-Mexican-American that we have today in northern New Mexico.

After the river heads south from Alamosa, it meanders through marshes of alkali flats and becomes the Alamosa National Wildlife Refuge. It becomes difficult to reach by road. Highway 142 from Manassa to San Luis was the road I took on one trip. At the Manassa bridge, I saw a man waist-deep in the river with instruments, calling out numbers to his partner onshore. I stopped and found out that they were computing the flow of water at that check station. The recorder explained that there are seven stations in Colorado, and each station is measured three times every month. Difficulties sometimes arise, however, because in January it is necessary to drill through two feet of ice. He noted that at the station on that day, approximately four hundred cubic feet of water were flowing through per second.

The man onshore went on to say that in 1968 the Supreme Court made a decision, known as the Rio Grande Interstate Compact, which allocated a certain percentage of the river's total water to each of the three states it flows through. This means that a close check is necessary to predict the total amount of water in order to ensure a fair allocation to the farms in the north. As a result, the official said, "It is a guessing game and a headache, because sometimes there is rain in October, and we can give the farmers more water when they don't need it."

He also pointed out that the Lobatos Bridge check station, south about six miles, was the last and most important gauging station because it was closest to New Mexico. "If you go there," he warned, "watch out for rattlesnakes. I saw three big ones under the bridge last time I was there." I did indeed go there because I have seven acres about one-fourth mile south of the Lobatos Bridge with about four hundred feet bordering on the river, and I wanted to revisit it. I saw no rattlesnakes (I did not go under the bridge). However, I did see a herd of pronghorns, sometimes called antelopes, and many jackrabbits in the vicinity.

I also found an Indian petroglyph, a plus sign enclosed in a six-inch circle scratched onto the rock. On that trip I waded and swam across the slow-moving, cold water and found a profusion of designs etched into the rocks on the western side. I climbed a treeless hill and investigated an abandoned mine tunnel. This area appeals to me because of its remoteness: on a busy day, one vehicle per hour might cross the Lobatos Bridge.

About six miles north of the New Mexico border, it connects

the gravel road from Antonito to Costilla. At the bridge the cliffs rise about twenty feet. This is the beginning of the Rio Grande Gorge. It is difficult to drive to the New Mexico border where the river crosses, but I finally made it over dirt "roads" and over no roads at all. The canyon on the border is about thirteen hundred feet wide and two hundred feet deep.

At the border, a tired, depleted river is reborn with springs and creeks and prepares for the difficult task of slicing through the Taos Plateau, which results in the spectacular Rio Grande Gorge of New Mexico.

1. The Source

A permanent snowbank rests like a saddle on top of Stony Pass, high on the Continental Divide. This is the official source of the Great River, the Rio Grande. Small alpine flowers grew profusely, and water was everywhere. I kept thinking of *The Sound of Music*. After ten minutes of painting, I noticed I was sitting in a puddle of ice water. The permafrost was melting. The rocks were sharp, and the sky was blue.

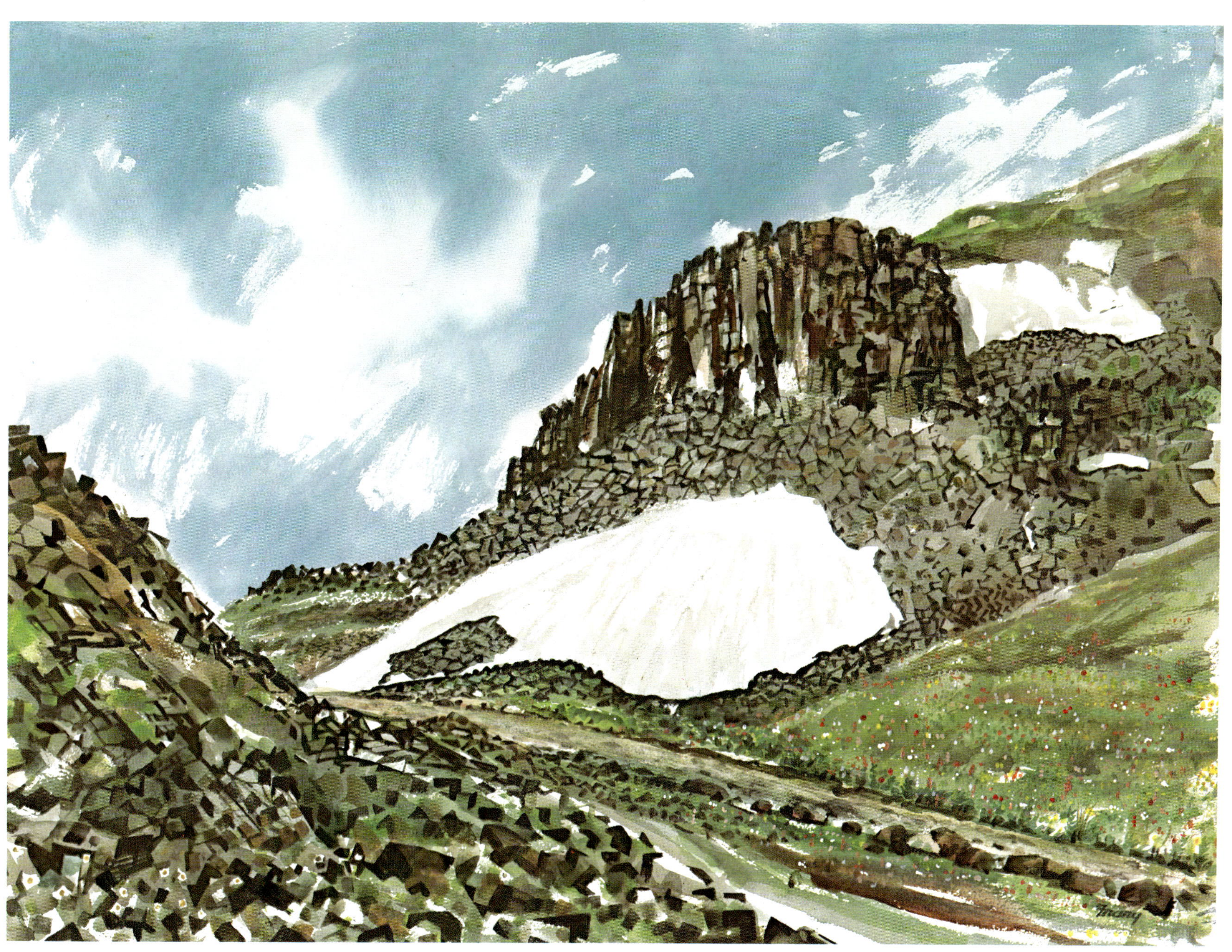

2. Rio Grande Pyramid

The Rio Grande Pyramid is one of the many pyramidal-shaped peaks thirteen thousand to fourteen thousand feet high marking the Continental Divide in this area of the incomparable San Juan Mountains. This peak is about six miles from the Rio Grande Reservoir and Lost Trail Creek campgrounds.

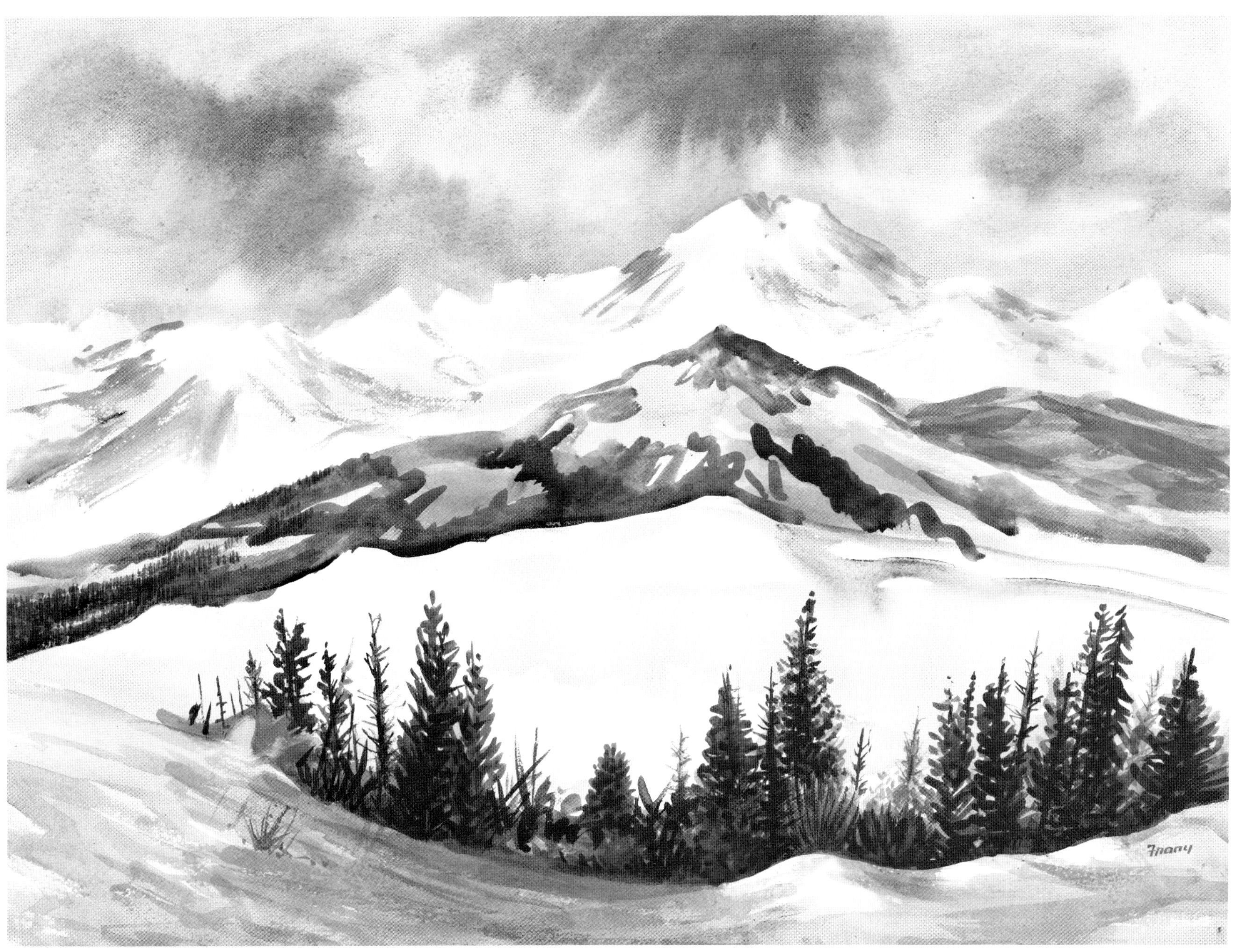

3. Englemann Spruce and Snow-capped Peaks

I did this quickly on a cold day. Sometimes a rapid, spontaneous effort in watercolor gives a more expressive feeling of the place than does a detailed study.

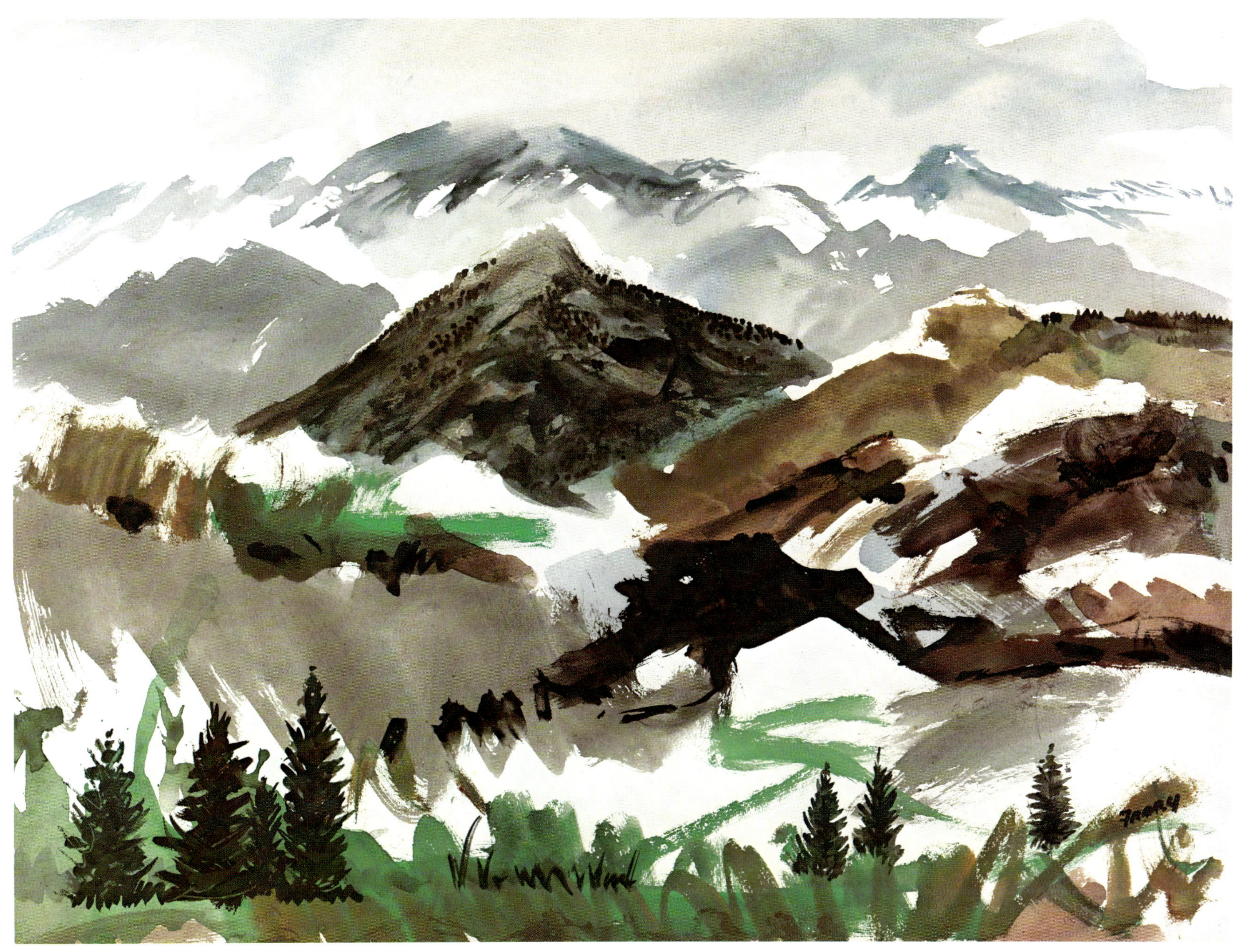

4. Fifteen Degrees

I did this painting in fifteen-degree weather. Soon after I brushed on a wash the water froze, and because of the low humidity the ice evaporated, leaving the pigments in an ice-crystal pattern. I thought that I had discovered a new technique, but found out later that others had done it before. I could not paint with gloves on and had to defrost my hands, palette, and brush every few minutes.

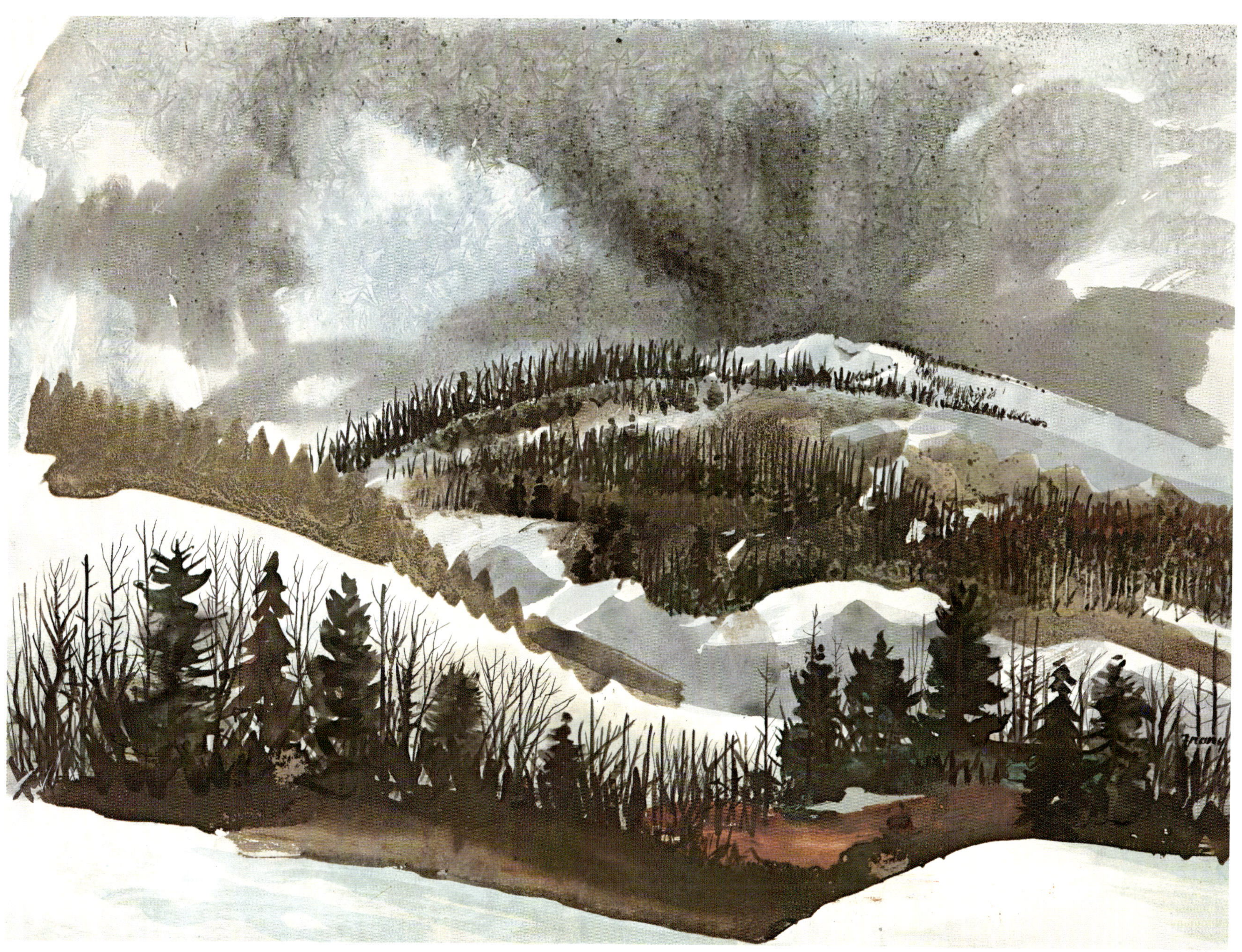

5. Lost Trail Creek

While I was painting from the bridge over Lost Trail Creek, a group of backpackers arrived. They took off their boots and put their feet in the icy water, whereupon each one began massaging his or her partner's feet. They had backpacked from Wolf Creek Pass along the Continental Divide, then down from Stony Pass to here. The confluence of Lost Trail Creek and the Rio Grande is just about as high on the pass as you can go in a two-wheel-drive vehicle. After this, Stony Pass lives up to its name.

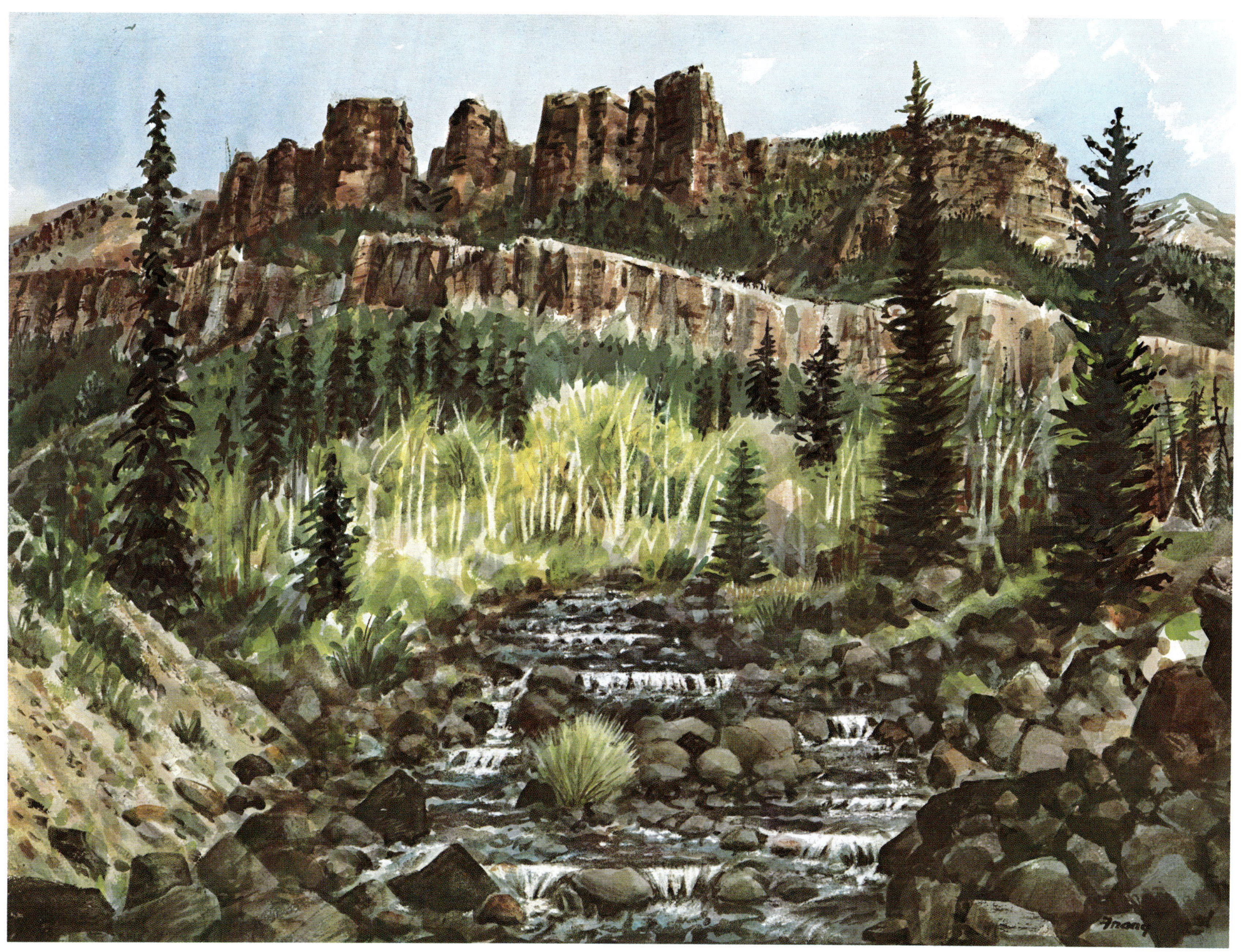

6. Castles above Lost Trail Creek Campgrounds

Directly above Lost Trail Creek campgrounds are burnt sienna outcroppings aptly named "castles." One of the problems here was to paint the negative dark shapes and leave the positive white paper to define the contours of the foreground foliage. Another problem was that it started to rain—note the drops of water in the sky area. I have painted under and withstood difficult circumstances such as heat, cold, wind, ants, mosquitoes, and crowds, but I have found that if it begins to rain, it is best to get under cover.

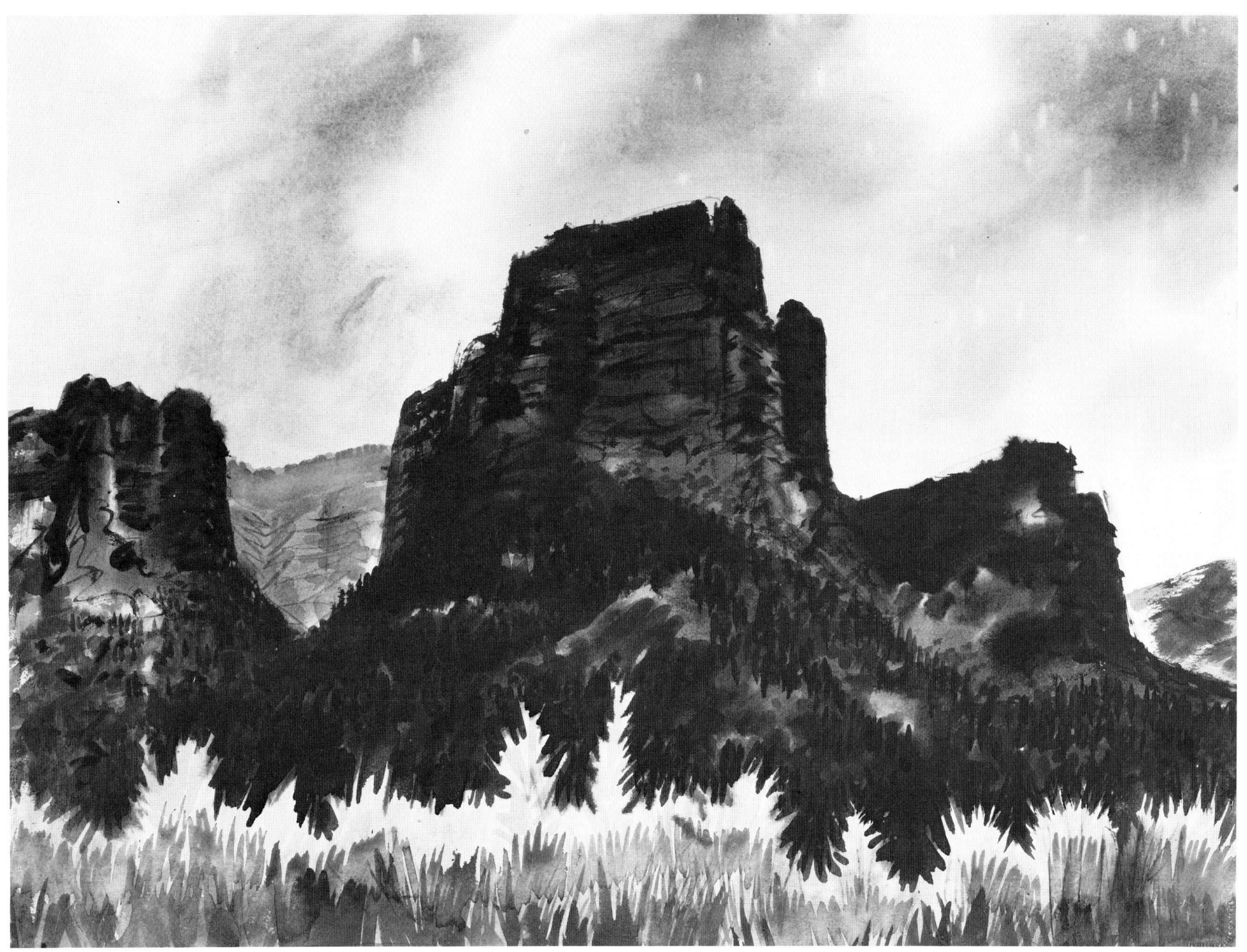

7. Aspen in the Fall

The aspen is a type of poplar tree with flattened leafstalks that cause the leaves to flutter in the least breeze. The other trees here, mainly needle leaf, remain dark green while clumps of aspen change from green to yellow to gold to red throughout the year. October is considered one of the preferred months to observe these high-altitude color transformations.

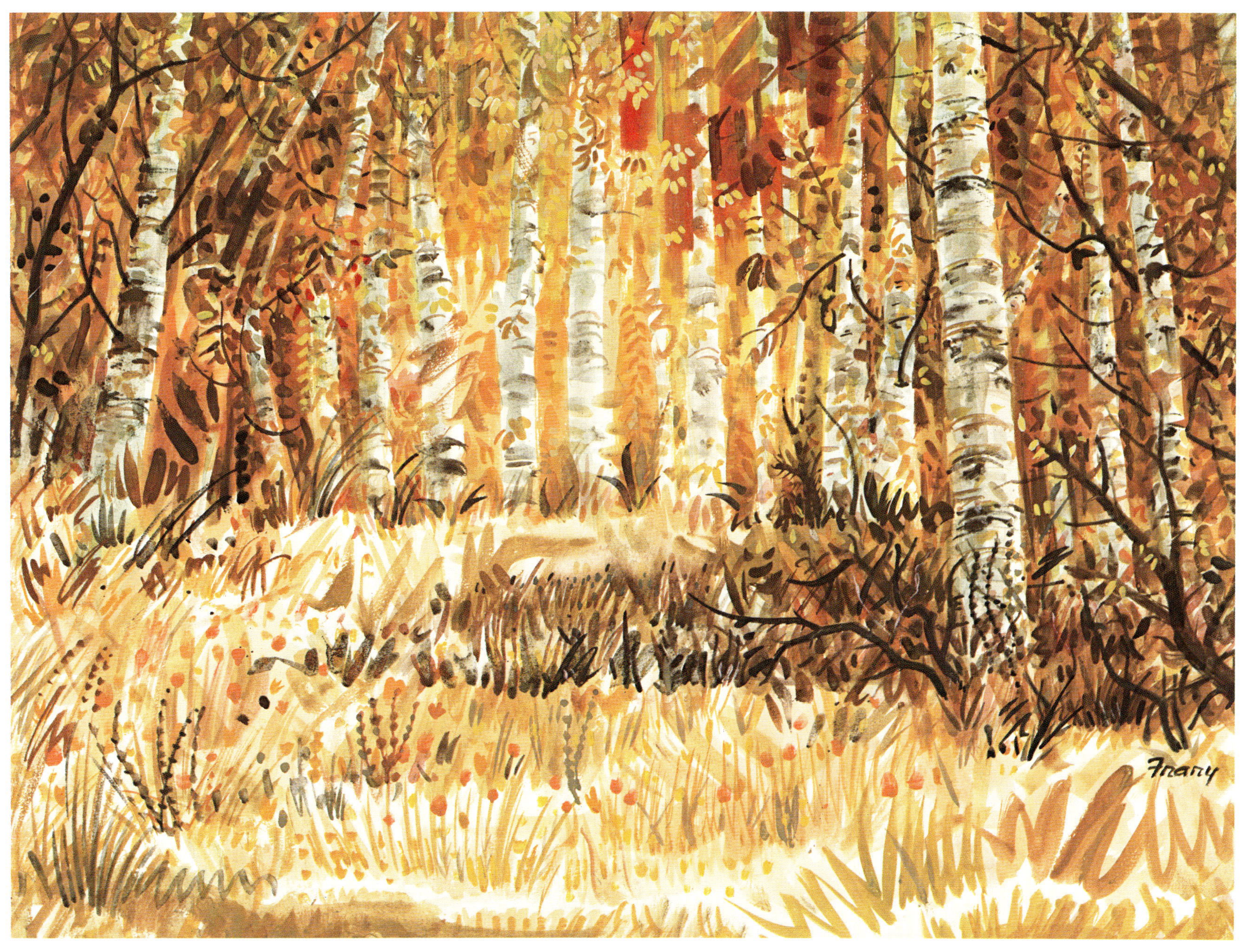
Frany

8. Castle Rock Lake

There are many small, narrow lakes and reservoirs on both sides of the Rio Grande in the upper Rio Grande Valley. Castle Rock Lake is north of Finger Mesa and is actually composed of several small lakes. It helps to have a four-wheel-drive vehicle in this area.

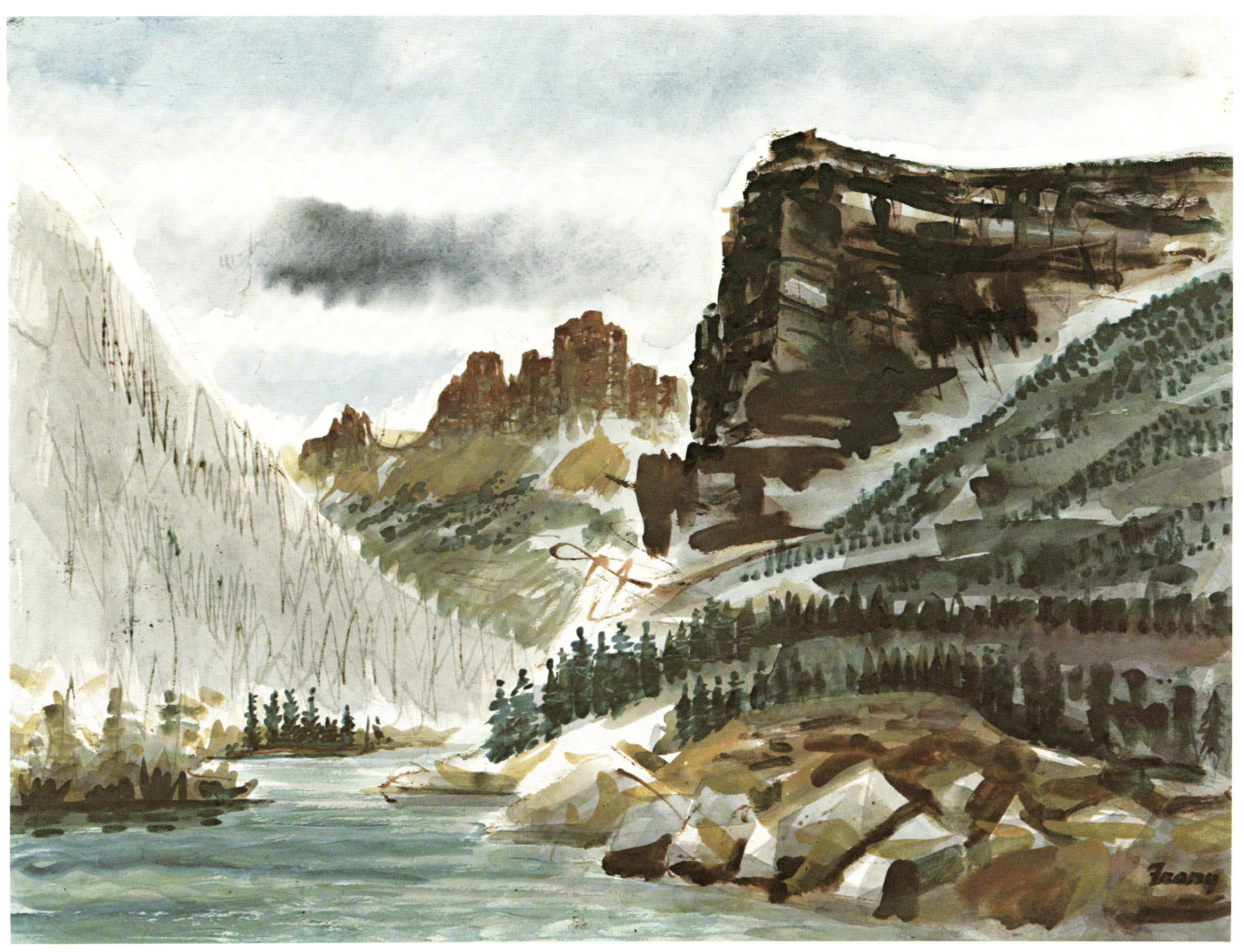

9. Rio Grande Reservoir

This earthen dam is the first control of the Rio Grande. The reservoir thus formed provides the ranchers and farmers downstream with a steady flow of water all year long. I did this painting while sitting on the dam looking upstream. A summer storm came up, and the wind blew cold and strong.

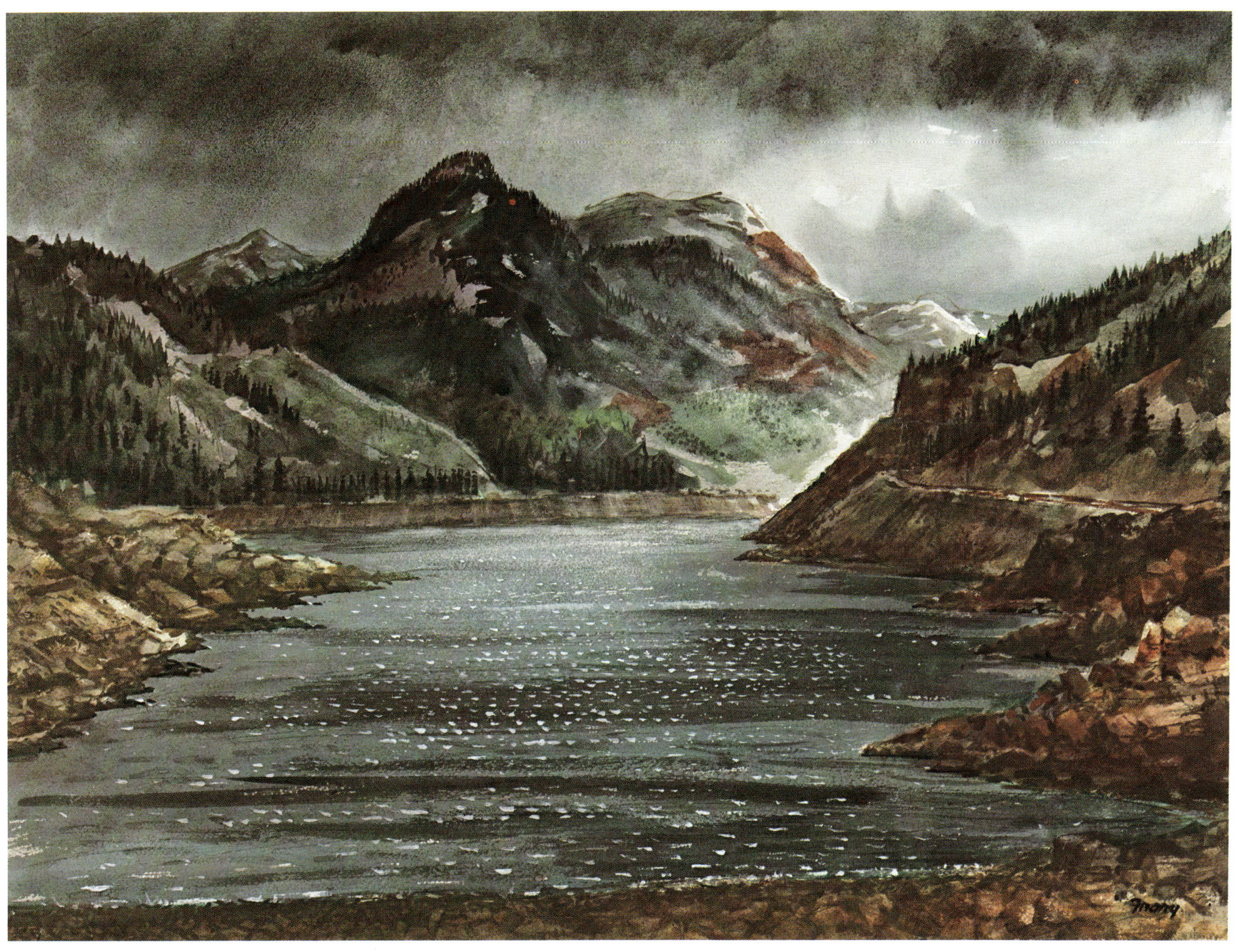

10. Near Bristol Head

Bristol Head is a massive upthrust visible for many miles in the upper valley. The now-controlled river cascades down the slope. The trout fishing is considered excellent from the dam downstream for fifty miles.

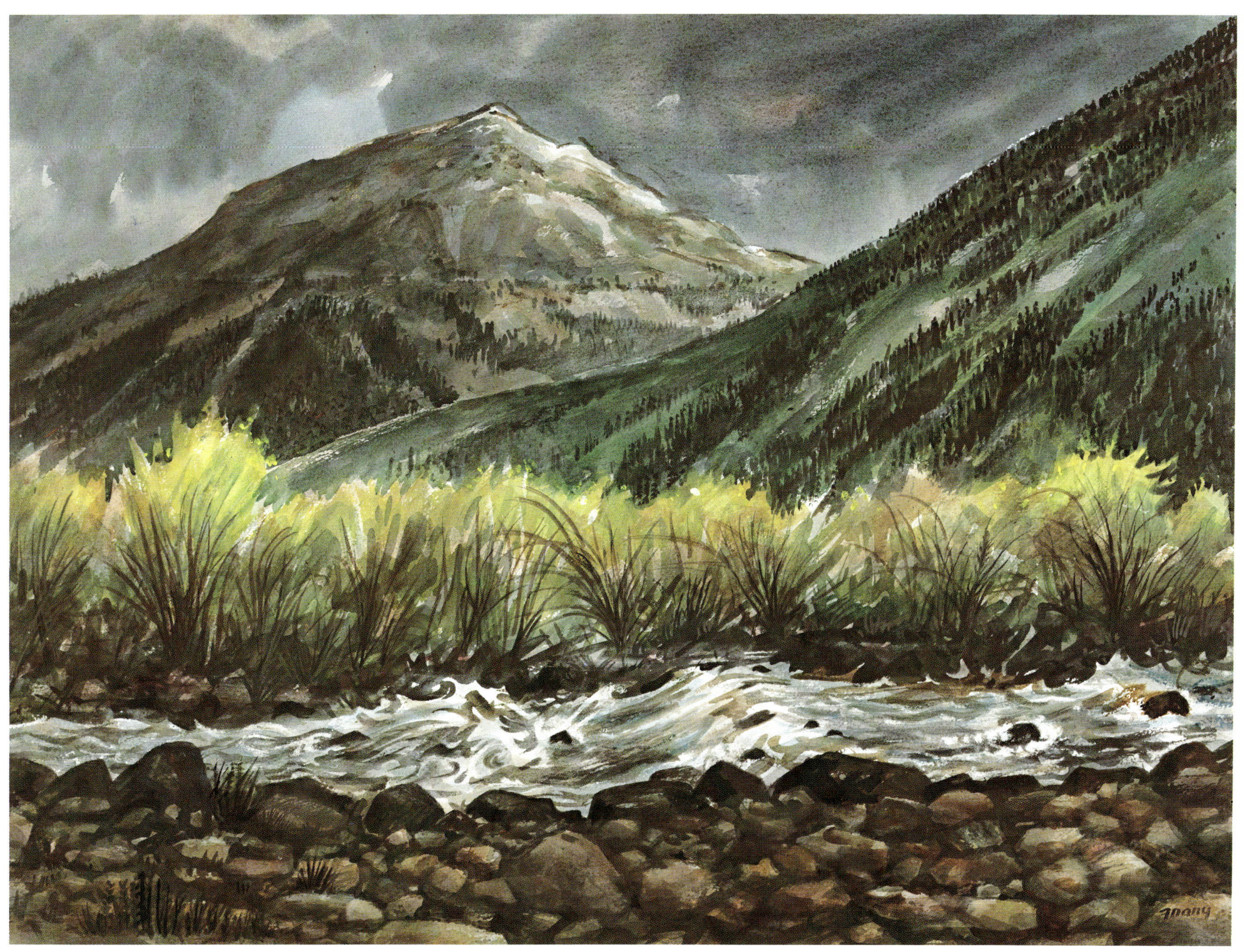

11. Old Mine Structure near Creede

The area around Creede was and still is an important mining center. Old structures like this are to be found in sometimes almost inaccessible locations. I thought that this old mine was particularly impressive and worthy of painting in detail. I added the dark cliff in back to make the forward thrust of the building more solid.

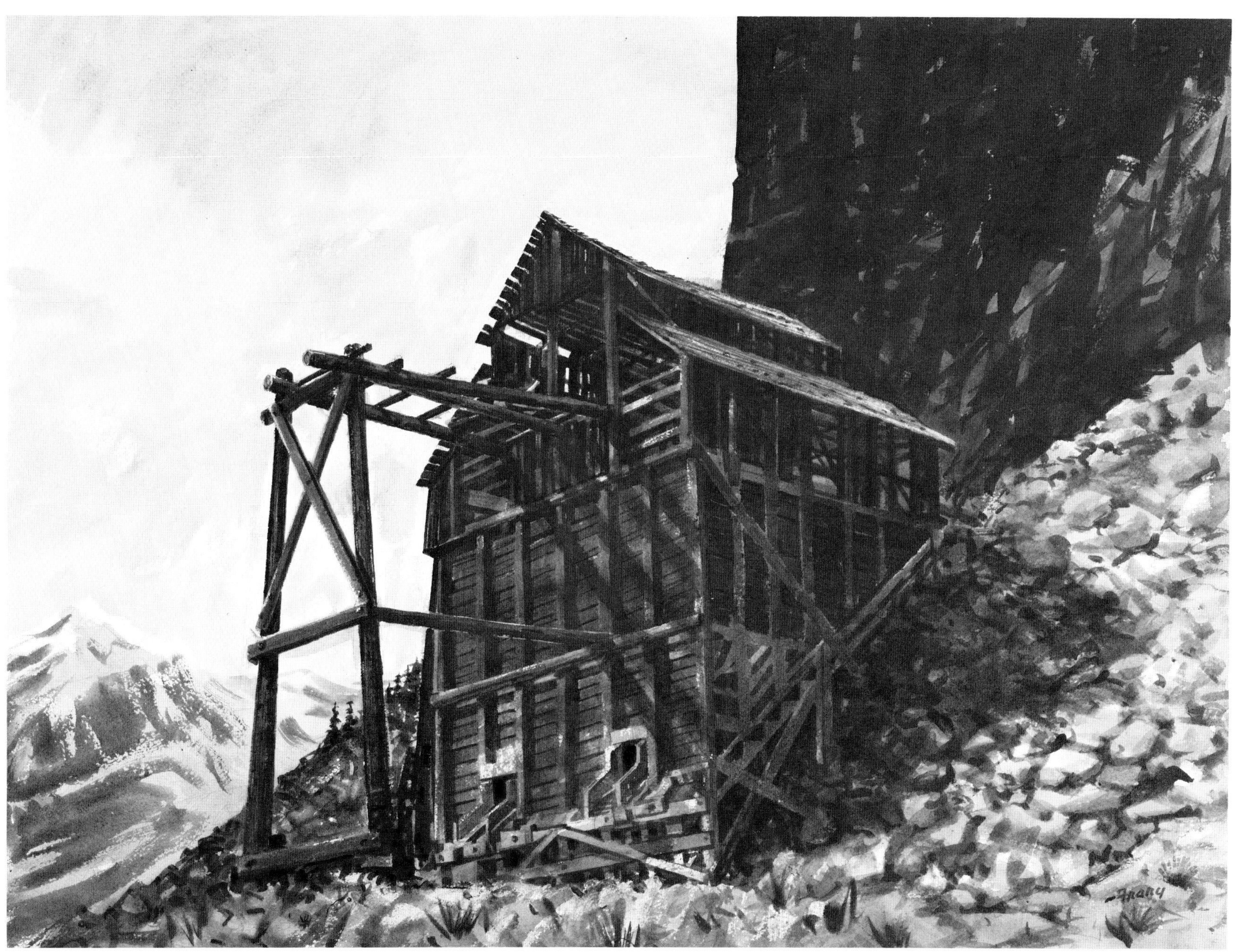

12. Downtown Creede

Creede is the metropolis of the upper Rio Grande Valley, with a current population of about three hundred fifty. In 1892 it was a wild boom town of ten thousand inhabitants, who came west by the trainload. Today everyone has a pickup truck. Residents include miners, shopkeepers, and sportsmen, with a steady sprinkling of tourists.

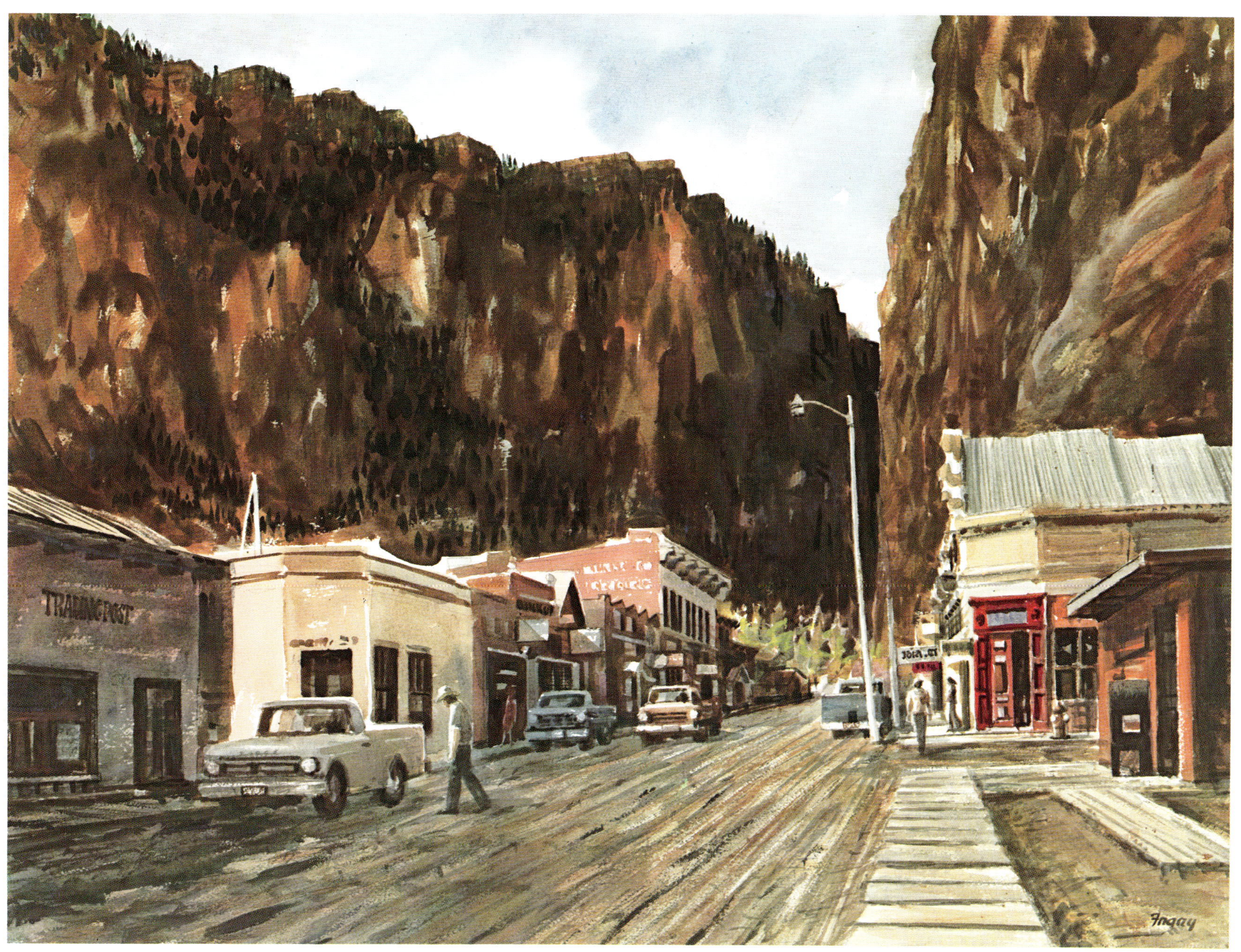
TRADING POST

13. Easy Run

The most important ski area in the upper Rio Grande region is at Wolf Creek Pass, thirty-eight miles south of Creede. Wolf Creek's average annual snowfall of 435 inches assures excellent skiing conditions from November through May. The drainage from this area forms the sizable South Fork River, which joins the Rio Grande at the town of South Fork.

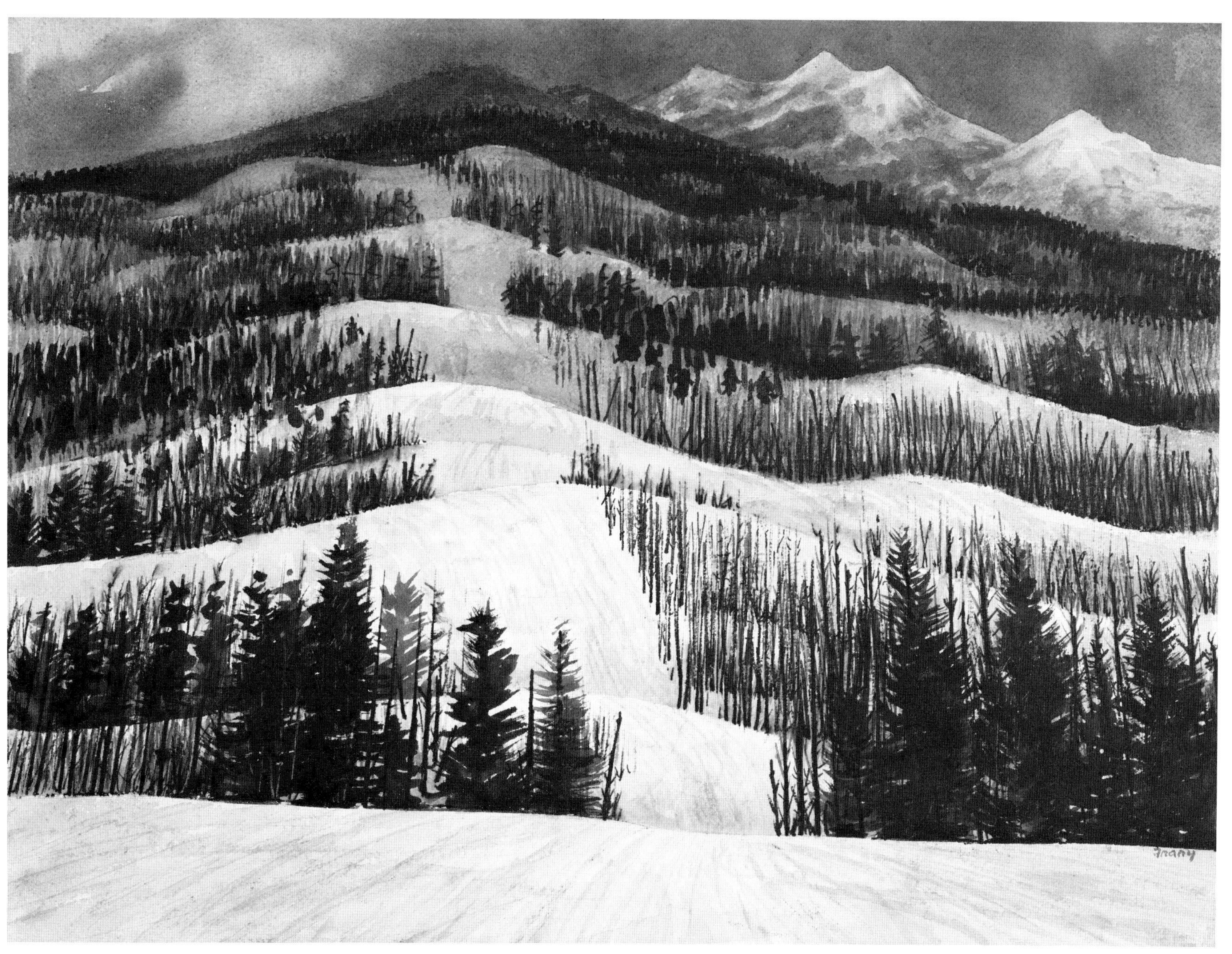

14. Wagon Wheel Gap

This was the last stop for the Denver and Rio Grande Railway, so important to Creede in the 1890s, before going upriver to Creede. The valley narrows here, cliffs converge on both sides, and cottonwood trees make their contribution to the seasonal changes in color throughout the year.

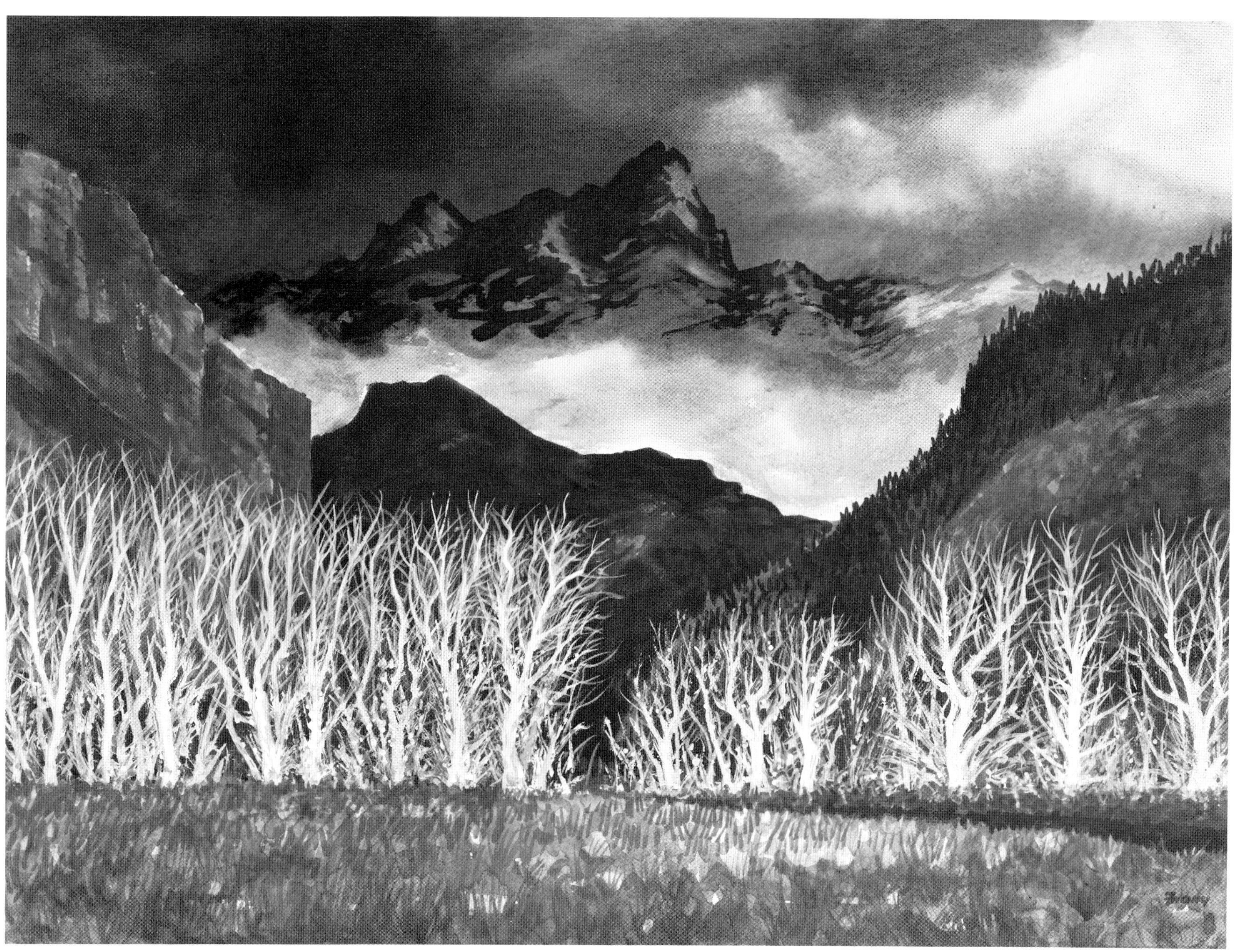

15. Irrigating with Siphon Tubes near Monte Vista

The Rio Grande has turned hundreds of square miles of high-altitude desert into productive farmland. The towns of Del Norte, Monte Vista, and Alamosa exist because of the river. Almost all of Colorado's total water allocation goes into the canal system of the north San Luis Valley.

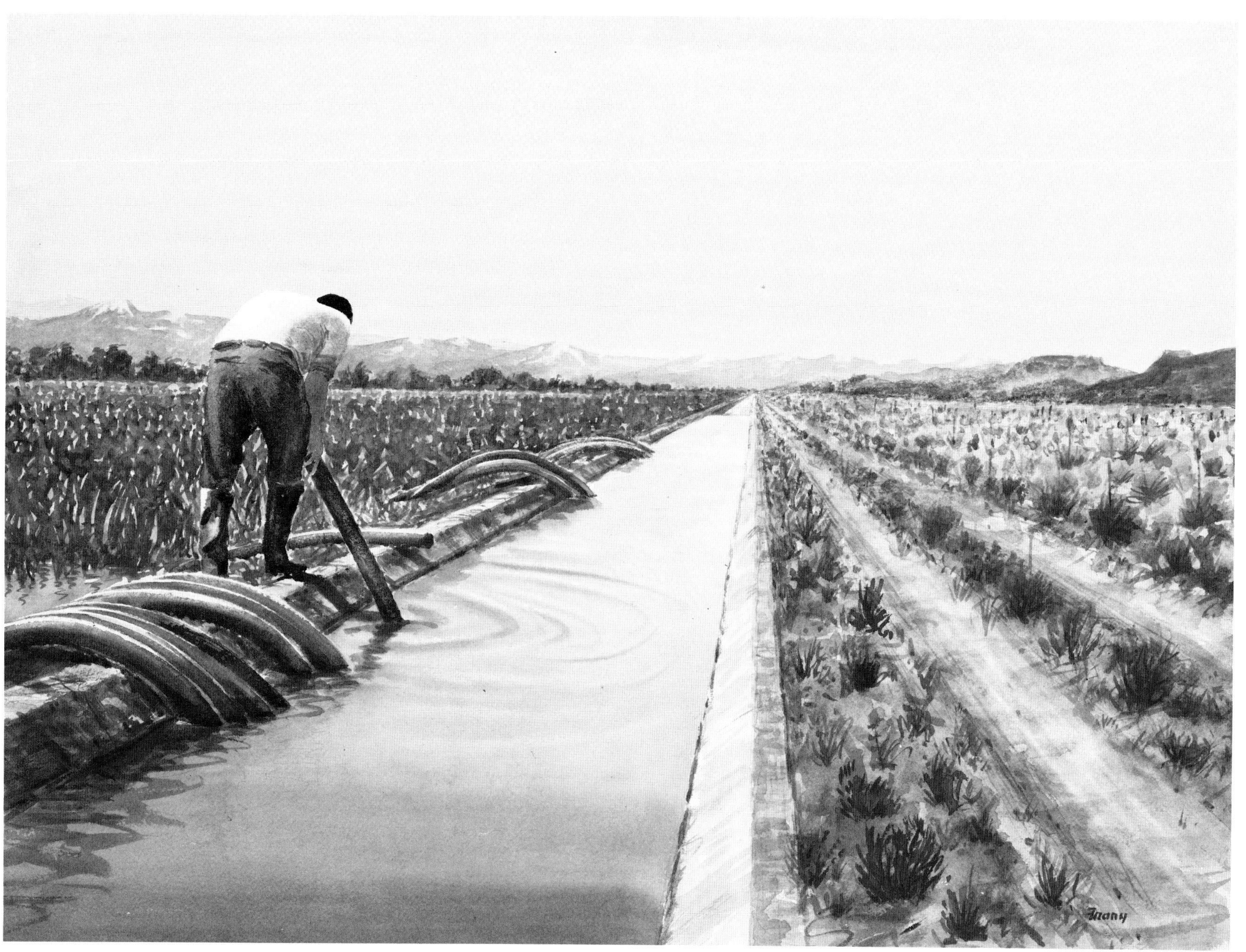

16. Manassa Bridge Check Station

This man was determining the total flow of the river at the check station, a task performed three times a month at each of seven check stations in Colorado. This computation makes it possible to divide the river's total water into percentages allocated to the states governed by the Supreme Court's Rio Grande Interstate Compact. There is a growing concern to conserve water and use it efficiently.

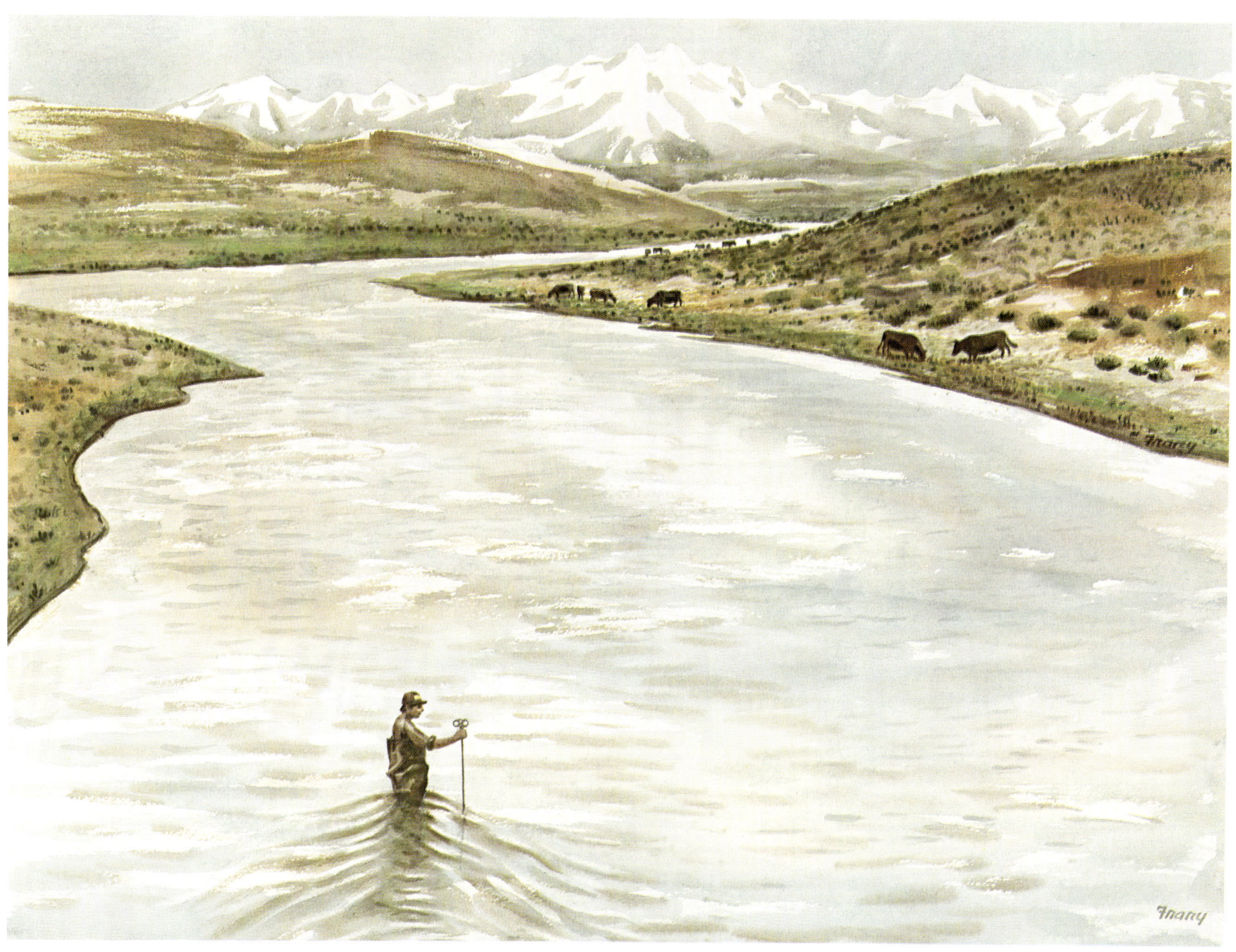

Part Two: The New Mexico Rio Grande

The New Mexico Rio Grande

The Rio Grande bisects New Mexico from north to south, bordered by mountains all the way. The Sangre de Cristos, Sandias, Manzanos, San Andres, Jemez, Gallinas, San Mateos, Black Range, Mimbres, and others follow each other on both sides of the river. In New Mexico the Rio Grande skirts the west side of Ute Mountain, a treeless, black, extinct volcano that rises to over ten thousand feet and forms the southern boundary of the San Luis Valley. The Ute Butte, as it is also called, is a massive cone that projects three thousand feet from the surrounding flat plain. Sometimes, when the snow is melting, the contrast between the black cinder rocks and the white snow is spectacular.

From the border south the gorge deepens, and the rocky tumblings clean and invigorate the water. Many cold springs add to the size of the now-reborn primitive river. In 1970 this part of the river was the first in the United States to be named a Wild River by an act of Congress. The forty-eight miles south of the Colorado border plus the lower four miles of the Red River are now a nature preserve, offering memorable experiences to the hiker and fisherman and nightmares to the river runner. The twelve miles from Lee Crossing, soon after the river circles west of Ute Mountain, to the junction of Red River are rated grade six: "utmost difficulty—near limit of navigability." A ranger told me that three weeks ago, four men put in their raft at Lee Crossing and only one man survived. The Wild River area is one of the spectacular extremes of this many-faceted river.

There is a good campground at the confluence of the Rio Grande and the Red River. The Red River coming in from the east has an eight-hundred-foot-deep gorge of its own to meet the Rio Grande.When I stood on the overlook, I felt as if I were standing on the bow of a great ocean liner. I looked almost straight down and saw V-shaped patches of white in both rivers where the heavy mass of water was surging over, around, and under house-sized boulders. I felt the vibration and heard the distant rumble. Good trails lead to the bottom. I hiked down to Big Arsenic Springs, where ninety gallons of pure icy water per second rush into deep pools in which ten-pound trout have been caught. Down below, with the incessant roar of the water pounding and churning on the rocks, I sensed the incredible power of surging water. Spray covered the rocky banks and the lush vegetation. This is another world. The presence of the Great River dominated my senses, and I felt that I was close to the heart of the Rio Grande.

About eight miles downstream from the Red River junction, the Rio Hondo tumbles in joyfully from the east. The cut in the lava flows made by this small river allows automobiles to cross the Rio Grande on the John Dunn Bridge for the first time since Lobatos Bridge. As I was painting this bridge, I thought how peaceful and inviting the water looked. Then I spotted a sign on the other side that warned, "River Runners Caution: Extremely Dangerous Rapids Ahead."

From the bridge south for seventeen miles to Taos Junction Bridge the river is wild, almost inaccessible, and has a rating of five. It is called the Box because of walls that loom six to eight hundred feet above the river. The Box is considered the third most difficult one-day raft trip in any river in the United States. The difficulty varies at different times of the year because of the changing amounts of water pounding through the narrow passages. In an average winter, the river runs at a rate of perhaps four hundred cubic feet per second. During some springs, however, there may be twenty times that amount.

About four miles south of John Dunn Bridge, the Rio Grande Gorge Bridge spans two thousand feet across the canyon and rises six hundred feet above the water. After the high bridge come the really big drops in the river—Ski Jump, Dead Car, Power-Line Falls, Rock Garden, and other infamous rapids—which provide some of the heaviest wild water in the United States. There are foaming drops, huge boulders, hydraulics, whirlpools, and other dangers that severely test the most experienced river runners. The end of the run, the end of the U.S. Wild River area, is at Taos Junction Bridge. The Taos Creek comes in at this point. After the bridge, the river immediately changes its character: the canyon widens abruptly, allowing room for a road and livestock. I have camped along this road to Pilar several times, and I like the area. The now-tame river and the cattle grazing along the banks produce a pastoral setting that is completely different from the churning rapids a short distance upstream or downstream.

The first use of the water for irrigation since the San Luis Valley in Colorado is at Pilar, where it is channeled onto a few acres of vegetable gardens and fruit trees. From Pilar to Rinconada the river drops down a stretch of rapids rated expert grade four, then drifts past a snug, verdant valley called Velarde, where the orchards of fruit trees and fields of chili are irrigated by three ditches off the river and have been for hundreds of years.

The Rio Grande drifts slowly down past the confluence of the Rio Chama, past the town of Española, past pueblos with orchards and vegetable gardens to the end of the Española Valley, to the Otowi Bridge and White Rock Canyon.

This whole region of north-central New Mexico is extremely important historically. The Spanish colonial towns on the high road from Taos to Santa Fe represent one of the oldest centers of civilization in the United States. Las Trampas, Truchas, Chimayo, and other isolated mountain villages remain much as they were three hundred years ago, except that some of the buildings now sport shiny tin roofs. In some towns, the Spanish of Cervantes's time is still spoken, such as, "¿Cómo estamos?" instead of "¿Cómo está usted?" ("How are we?" instead of "How are you?").

As old as these Spanish colonial towns are, a much older civilization remains in isolated communities nearer the Rio Grande. Nineteen Pueblo Indian groups are now included in the census of New Mexico. They are almost equally divided north and southwest from Santa Fe. The Pueblo Period began around A.D. 400 with the development of "pit-houses." Today each pueblo (village or town) has its own individual characteristics, and many of the Pueblo Indians are becoming noted for their fine crafts.

As early as twenty thousand years ago, well before the Pueblo Indians, man inhabited the middle valley of the Rio Grande. These Paleo-Indian–Stone Age hunters produced points for spears and arrows, world famous for their craftsmanship. The climate became warmer about 6000 B.C., prompting a shift from a meat to a vegetable economy. This development, from 6000 B.C. to A.D. 1, has been named the Archaic Period. Corn appeared in this valley about two thousand years ago. This was very important because it made possible a food surplus, which in turn fostered communal living along the middle valleys of the Rio Grande. By A.D. 1000 these people lived peacefully and democratically, while Europe was torn by the bloody savagery of the Dark Ages.

Corn was and still is the Indians' physical and spiritual staple; the conservation of water, a sacred trust. This reverence for water is possibly traceable to their ancestors, the Anasazis ("old ones"), who settled in the region about A.D. 1250. The Anasazis, who had suffered many years of drought in the Mesa Verde country to the west, were overjoyed to find abundant supplies of water near the Rio Grande. This feeling of gratitude has been passed down from generation to generation as a sacred heritage.

Today Blue Lake, the source of Taos Creek, is the most sacred shrine of the Indians living at Taos Pueblo. This pueblo is the largest in the area, with a population of about two thousand and two large adobe building complexes of five stories each. Picuris (pee-kuhr-rees′), between Taos and Santa Fe, is the smallest, with two hundred inhabitants. This little pueblo, hidden in the mountains, is my favorite. One day I was sitting on the ground next to a large new motor home that I had rented and was painting the adobe church. A strong and stern-looking man, obviously a local Indian, came up and watched me work. I was rather apprehensive because some pueblos have strict regulations forbidding photographing, drawing, or painting the premises. After a few tense moments, he said, "I don't have any talent myself, but my aunt paints." My apprehension turned to relief. After a short conversation he asked, "Do you have any trouble with the generator on your R.V.?" I admitted that I was indeed having trouble with it. He replied, "I've been having trouble with mine. I have the same model as this. Maybe it is the altitude." My relief turned to astonishment.

Picuris has a small museum that houses local crafts and artifacts. A few Picuris women go up the mountain to a secret place and pray to the Clay Lady to help them bring back some micaceous clay. The mica in the clay gives their pottery a distinctive sparkle. Their work is treasured by collectors.

Some pueblos are noted for their basketry, some for their pottery. One summer I went to the Santa Clara Pueblo to visit two friends, Grace Medicine Flower and Chief Joseph Lone Wolf, who are outstanding potters. When Mr. Lone Wolf told me that the Santa Clara Festival at the Puyé (puh-yeh′) cliff ruins was going on that day, my wife and I drove up to the ruins. It was hot and dusty. The next dance on the schedule was the rain dance; when it ended, rain dutifully began to fall. The next dance was the buffalo dance. By this time I was convinced and expected to see some buffalo appear, but none did.

Each pueblo has its own dances and customs and is independent from all other pueblos. Pueblo history is fascinating. I had not known before I began this study that the first American Revolution occurred here. The Pueblo Indians were and are peaceful and have long maintained a closely knit social organization. In the seventeenth century, the hostile, hungry Mescalero Apaches of the mountains and the Kiowa-Comanches of the plains raided the Pueblos with ferocity. The Spanish, however, were the eventual conquerors of the Pueblo Indians. The twenty-five hundred Spanish around Santa Fe in 1670 ruled with an iron hand and treated the Indians like slaves. They allowed no religious freedom; violators were executed or otherwise mistreated.

A leader arose named Po-pe, who had great organizational ability and surprising military skills. Po-pe coordinated the many different pueblos, fed misinformation to the Spaniards, and waited until the propitious moment arrived; then, on August 10, 1680, the northern pueblos struck in unison. The Spanish governor, Otermin, and some survivors held out in the Palace of Governors at Santa Fe. After a short siege, they broke out in desperation and fled through the Jornada del Muerto ("journey of the dead") to El Paso. Twelve years later, Don Diego de Vargas led a bloodless reconquest. He ruled with less cruelty and gave the Indians religious freedom. History is recorded by the victors; consequently, little else is known about the heroic Indians of the first American Revolution.

Both Santa Fe and Taos are old towns, rich with history. Today, both are very popular centers for artists and craftsmen. Dating from the late sixteenth century, the city of Santa Fe was the center of Spanish settlement, the capital of the province of New Spain, and eventually the terminal for the nineteenth-century trade route called the Santa Fe Trail. The unique city of Santa Fe, the oldest capital in the United States, is justly proud of its heritage and insists on reflecting the Indian-Spanish adobe architecture and way of life, as does Taos to the north. It did, however, give me a shock when I saw a McDonald's being constructed out of cement blocks and tin cylinders to represent adobe and wooden beams.

Santa Fe is about twenty miles east of White Rock Canyon. From Otowi Bridge southwest to Cochiti (koh′-chee-tee) Reservoir the river is rated grade four, and I heard that the scenery is spectacular there.

I met a friend in Santa Fe who said he could take me to the rim by driving directly west from the city. We drove on primitive roads, trails, and no trails over the Caja del Rio Plateau to the rim of the canyon. We arrived at the rim just upriver from where Frijoles Creek drains into the river, and we could see the clean little residential town of White Rock to the right across the river. The cliffs were indeed spectacular with their white volcanic pumice layered with streams of dark lava. It occurred to me that Santa Fe should develop some recreation sites in this area.

Downriver from the massive Cochiti Dam, the water passes through canals and ditches and irrigates the fields of the Cochiti, Santo Domingo, and San Felipe Indians. The church in Santo Domingo Pueblo has an interesting mural of horses painted on the facade. Most of the pueblos south of Santa Fe forbid picture taking, drawing, or painting.

I have stayed at the Coronado State Monument and Park near Bernalillo several times. Coronado, searching for the Seven Cities of Cibola, possibly wintered here on the riverbanks in 1540. This is the site of the ruins of Kuaua (kwa′-ah), Tiwa for "evergreen." There are many small rooms arranged around open plazas, which contained underground ceremonial chambers called kivas. The kiva here at Kuaua contained some of the finest examples of prehistoric murals to be found in North America; both human and animal forms are painted in a crisp, knowledgeable manner. The river, immediately adjacent to the ruins, continues on through Bernalillo to Albuquerque.

Albuquerque is New Mexico's largest city. Half a million people live in the area, and it is growing. The city is home for the University of New Mexico, and its biggest industry is nuclear research. The Rio Grande, approaching Albuquerque, has a broad, sandy bed lined with cottonwoods and willows. Sometimes the only flowing water is in the irrigation ditches and drains that parallel its bed. The ditch riders, mechanics directed by the water master, open the gates of the river and get the water running; it is then diverted to the feeder in the Albuquerque Main Canal. (The water master is in charge of all irrigation ditches, drains, and canals.) The canals fill up with sand, tumbleweed, chamiso, and coyote melon and are dredged every spring. The Cochiti Dam upstream is now easing the silting problem at Albuquerque, where the riverbed behind its levee rises as much as seven feet higher than city streets. I was told that as the population grows, housing developments will compete with farmers for water, which will eventually create a critical water shortage here and elsewhere in the Southwest Sunbelt.

The overtaxed water supply of the fourteen-hundred-mile-long Colorado River to the west has already posed serious difficulties for the entire nation and ultimately could trigger the biggest crisis in resources this country has yet experienced. The usual answer to the growing need for water is to build more dams for reservoirs to store water and for flood control. The problem is that water storage and flood control are mutually incompatible: water storage requires full reservoirs, while flood control demands empty ones. Another problem is that reservoirs lose their effectiveness in both respects by filling up with silt. On top of this, in most reservoirs the water evaporates and concentrates salt in the water, which is undesirable for either agricultural use or drinking. The usual solution is to maximize the short-term use of the water and spend more millions to correct the problems caused by the new engineering.

Below the main Albuquerque diversion, there is usually not enough water to maintain the flow of the river. To remedy this and to reduce the siltation, a channel has been dredged to help the river flow. A few miles south of Albuquerque the Isleta (ees-lay′-tah) Pueblo Indians have erected a dam, and the small downstream town of Belen usually does not have much surface water. The river nourishes the cottonwoods, willows, and tamarisk, but away from the river the flora are strictly desertlike. Creosote bush and desert grasses cover the eroded hills. After Belen the Rio Puerco and the Rio Salado, both usually dry, enter from the west. Beyond the town of Socorro, eighty miles south of Albuquerque, the Gallina Mountains push in from the west, and a narrow marsh is formed.

The Bosque del Apache ("woods of the Apaches") Wildlife Refuge, sometimes called the San Marcial Marshes, is home to thousands of waterfowl and other birds. The small farming town of San Marcial is now covered by sand dunes and salt cedars. Ironically, the town was destroyed by a flood caused by water backing up from a flood-control dam forty miles downstream. The huge Elephant Butte Dam, near the town of Truth or Consequences, was completed in 1916. The dam checks flooding downstream and delivers water to almost 300,000 acres, including the Rincon, Mesilla, El Paso, and Juárez valleys. There are frequent complaints from Mexico regarding water allocation, however, and the water deliveries must be constantly adjusted and adjudicated. The water from Elephant Butte is released into its holding basin, fifteen-mile-long Caballo ("horse") Lake. Just to the east of Elephant Butte and Caballo Lake lies the formidable valley of Jornada del Muerto. Appropriately, the world's first atomic bomb exploded here in 1945. The White Sands area, remarkable for its glistening white gypsum dunes, lies to the east.

On one painting trip, I was the only person to occupy any of the roofless campsites in the state park at Caballo Lake. Choosing one directly overlooking the water, I painted the lake and mountains to the east until the sun went down. After a while the full moon rose over the Caballo Mountains; I was so impressed that I kept on painting by moonlight. The next morning I was surprised when I saw my work. The values were all right, but the hues were not what I had intended. In one painting the sky was sepia (dark brown), and the mountain was blue. (Watercolorists should take note of this if they intend to paint by moonlight.)

The district south of the two large reservoirs is very productive. The small town of Hatch claims to be the chili capital of the world, while the Mesilla–Las Cruces area is the agricultural center of the Rio Abajo ("lower river"). Lettuce, onions, and pecans flourish, and the district is one of the nation's major sources of cotton. For a few miles, from Anthony to the famous El Paso del Norte, the river becomes the border between New Mexico and Texas. Anthony is unusual in that the border between Texas and New Mexico runs down the middle of the main street, causing problems because of different state laws. At this point the Rio Grande is wide and slow moving, ending its difficult voyage through New Mexico and preparing to irrigate eighty thousand acres in the El Paso Valley of Texas and over fifty thousand in the Juárez district of Mexico.

17. Looking South toward the Gorge

After the Colorado–New Mexico border, the river cuts deeper and deeper into the gorge. There are no roads to the river, but trails wind down from the eight-hundred-foot rim. Cattle may be seen going up and down the west slope on their narrow paths. It is interesting to notice their traffic control: one cow will wait at the relatively wide switchback for another one to go up or down a part that is too narrow for two to pass.

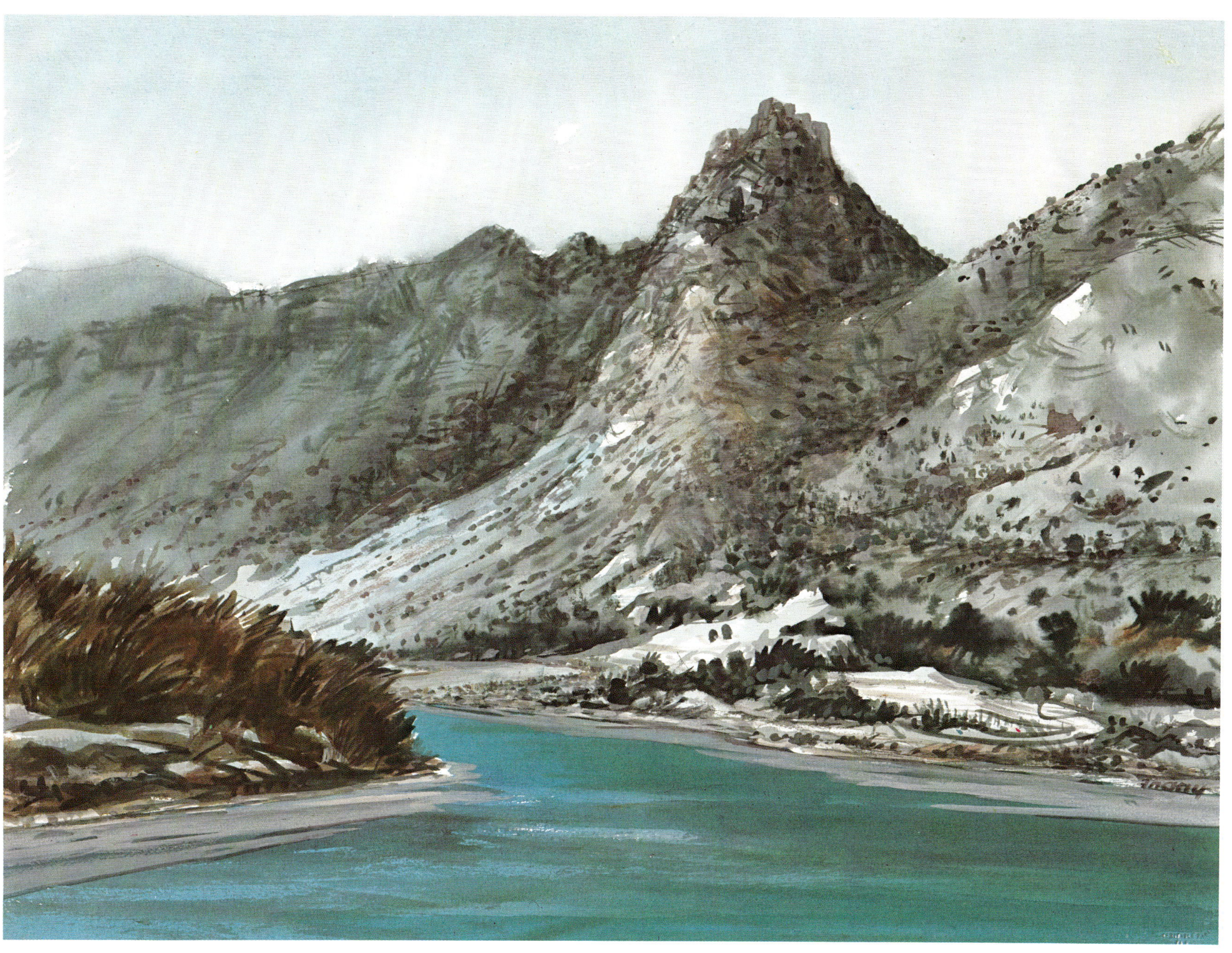

18. Near Big Arsenic Springs

The Wild River, depicted in August with low water, is refreshed by tumbling over rocks and by many springs such as Big Arsenic. This spring alone adds 5,400 gallons of pure icy water per minute to the Rio Grande. Fishermen consider this a paradise for ten-pound rainbow and brown trout.

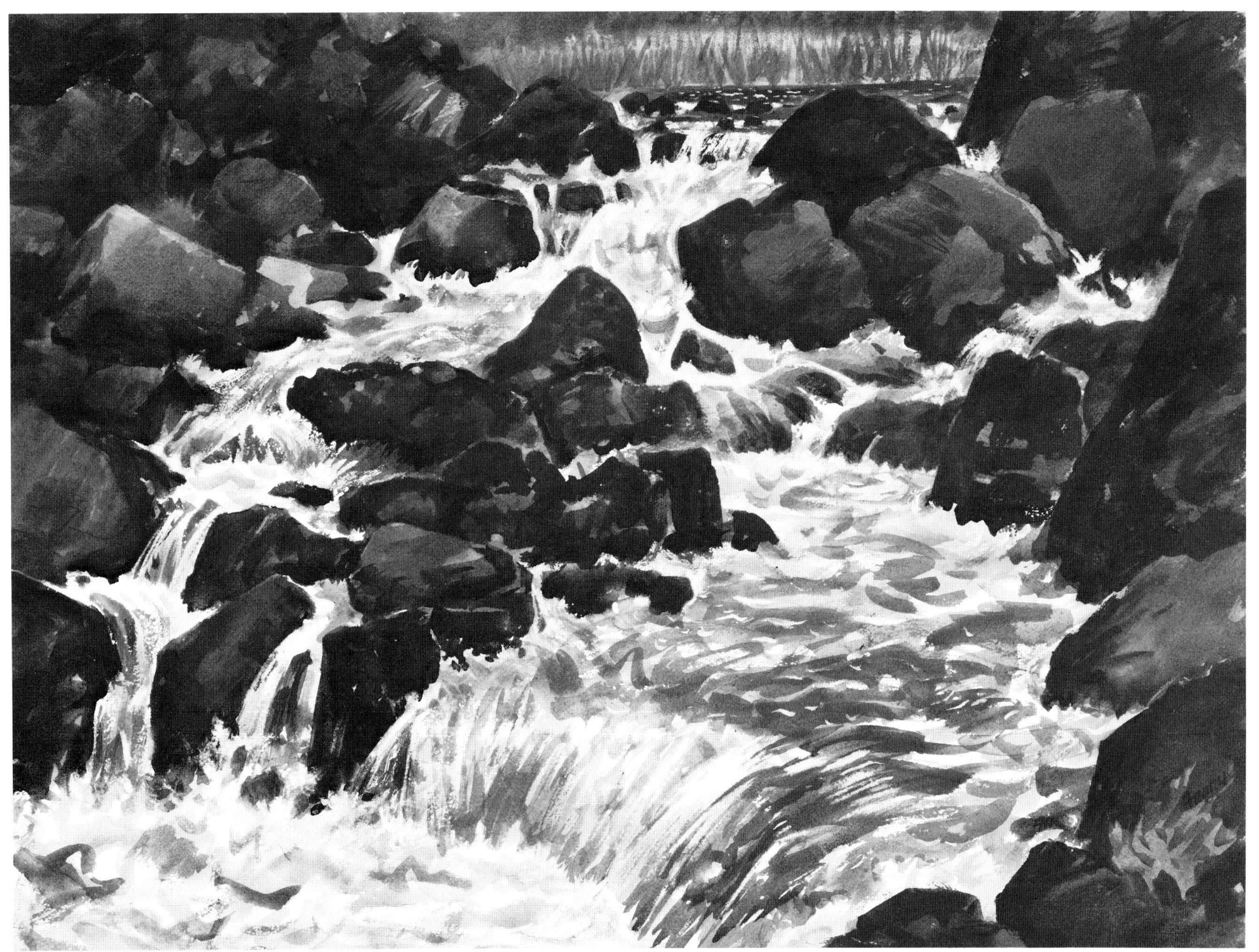

19. *John Dunn Bridge*

The Rio Hondo, as everyone writes, "tumbles in joyfully from the east." A road follows the Arroyo Hondo and crosses the Rio Grande here at the John Dunn Bridge. There are dangerous rapids downstream from the bridge. Two miles south are the remains of an old wagon road called La Bajada del Caballo, or "the descent of the horse." It is known today as Manby Springs.

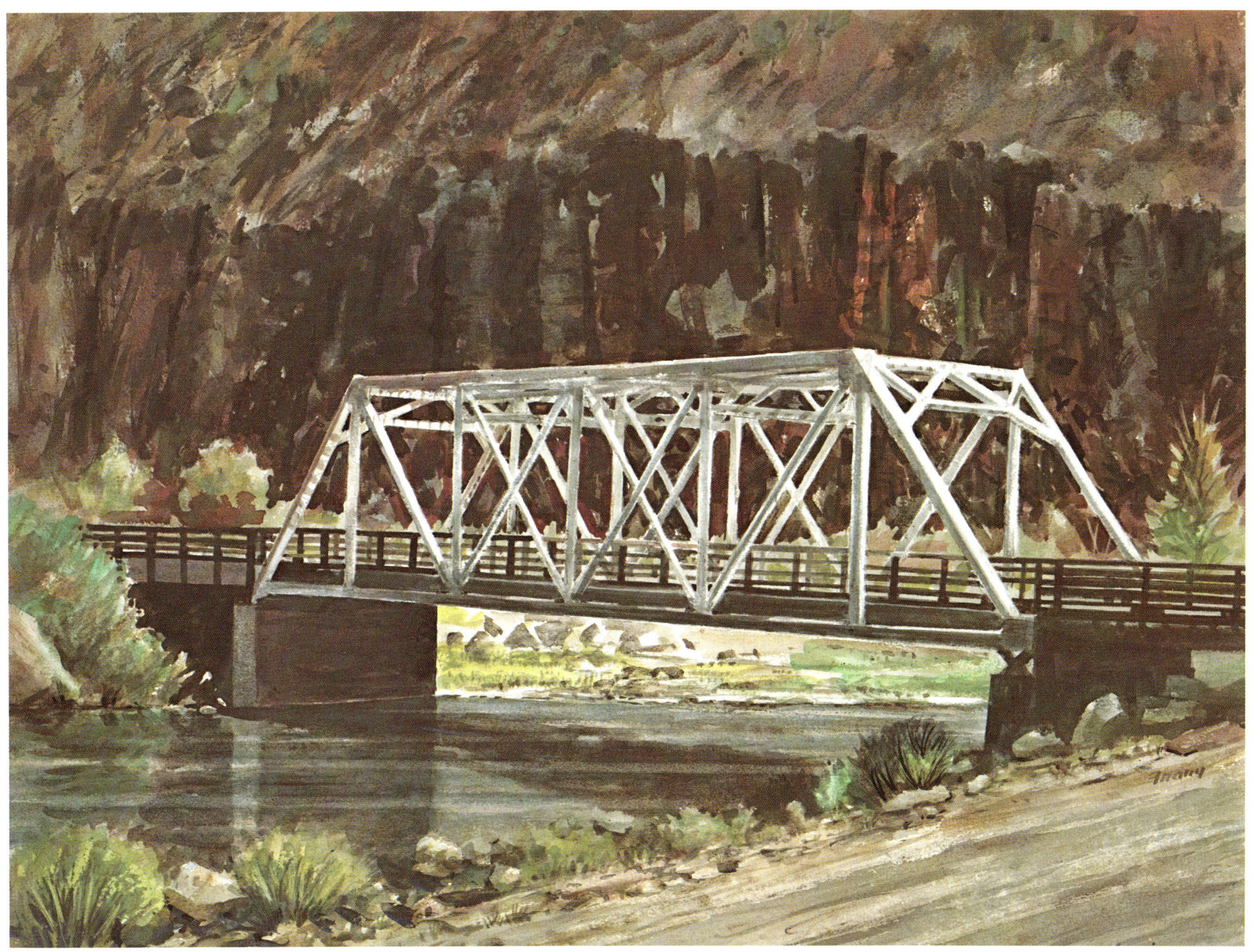

20. Buffalo above Taos Plateau

Driving from Taos west there is no indication of a river until you suddenly come to the Rio Grande Gorge Bridge. It is only from a higher elevation that the deep trench can be seen, and then only if the light is right. I added the buffalo because I thought it would be interesting to show how it was not so long ago.

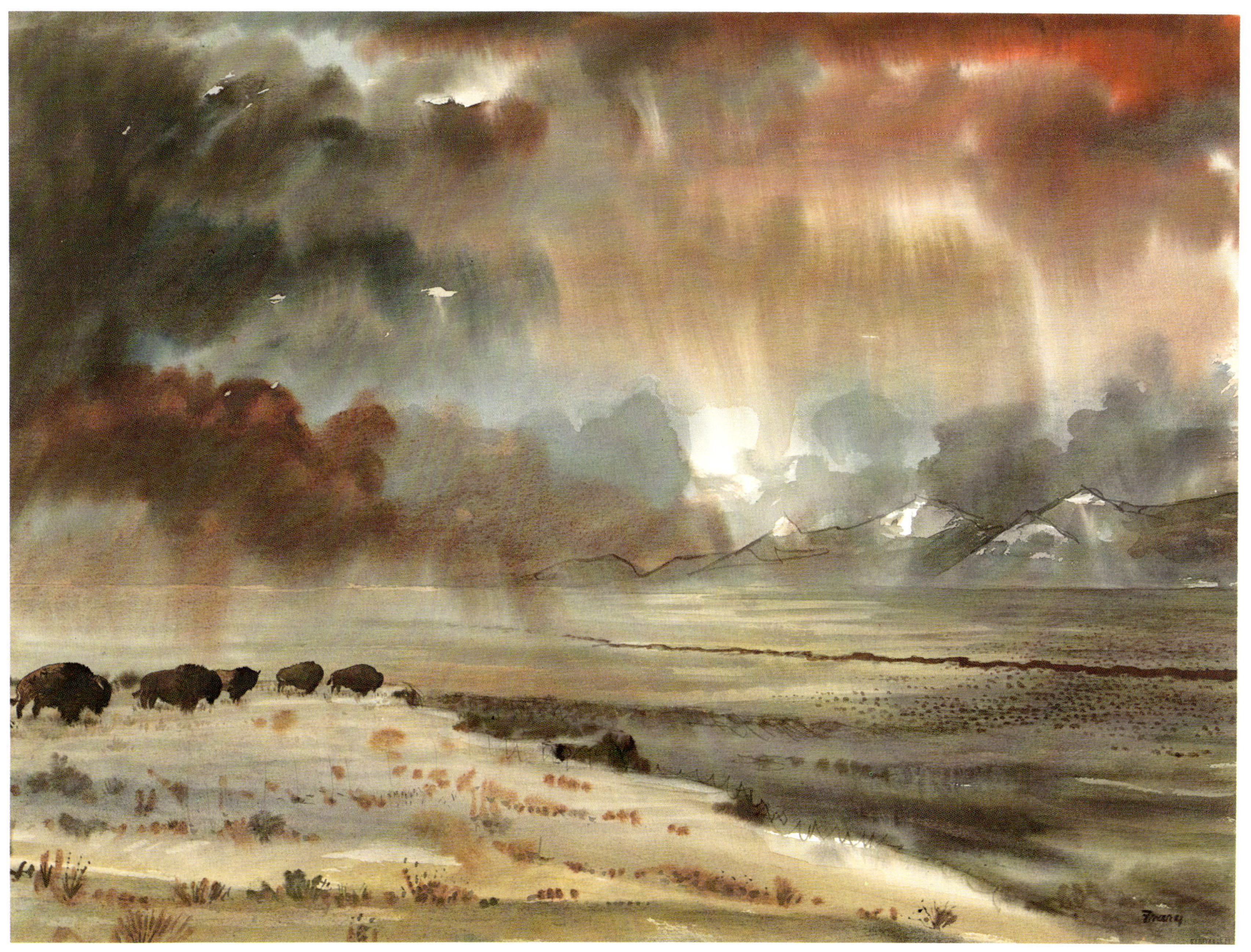

21. Rio Grande Gorge from the Bridge

From here to the end of the designated Wild River area at Taos Junction Bridge the Rio Grande is truly a wild river. This stretch is called the Box because of the surrounding cliffs, almost perpendicular and six to eight hundred feet high. Looking down from the height of the bridge, it is difficult to believe that foaming drops, whirlpools, hydraulics, and other extreme dangers to river runners exist. It is only when you listen to the distant roar, sense the vibration, and feel the moisture in a sudden updraft that you begin to sense the formidable power of the water.

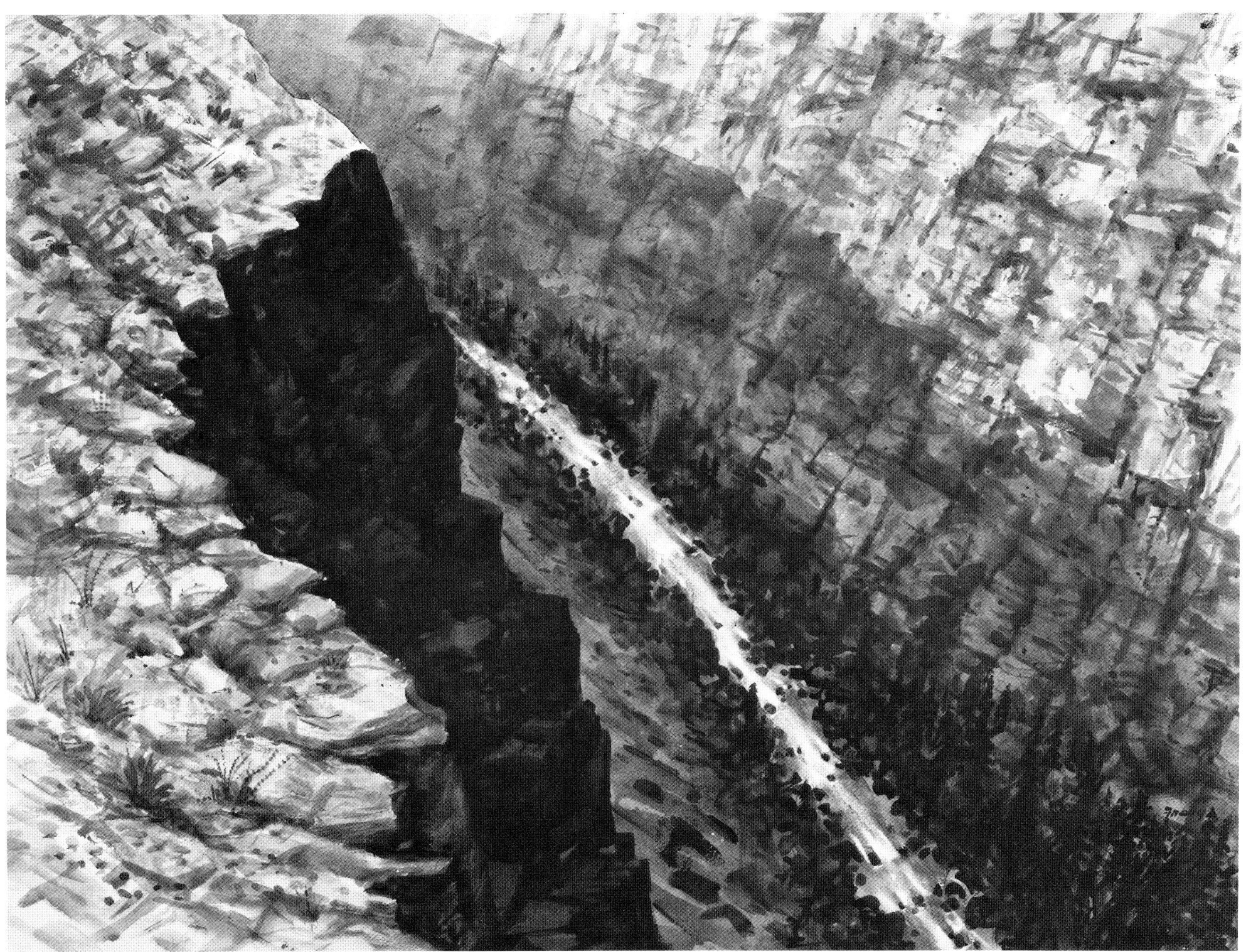

22. Taos Pueblo

With a population of about two thousand, Taos is the largest and the most widely known of the pueblos in this region. It has two large multistory dwelling units, with Taos Creek running constantly between the two. This painting represents the northern complex, looking up toward Blue Lake, the source of Taos Creek. I saw several men, dressed in gray cloaks with hoods, who reminded me of medieval monks. The Pueblo Indians have quietly gone about their peaceful daily activities seemingly undisturbed by the "civilizing" influence of first the Spanish conquerors, then the Mexican settlers, and now the American tourists. Three miles south of the pueblo is the historically and artistically famous town of Taos.

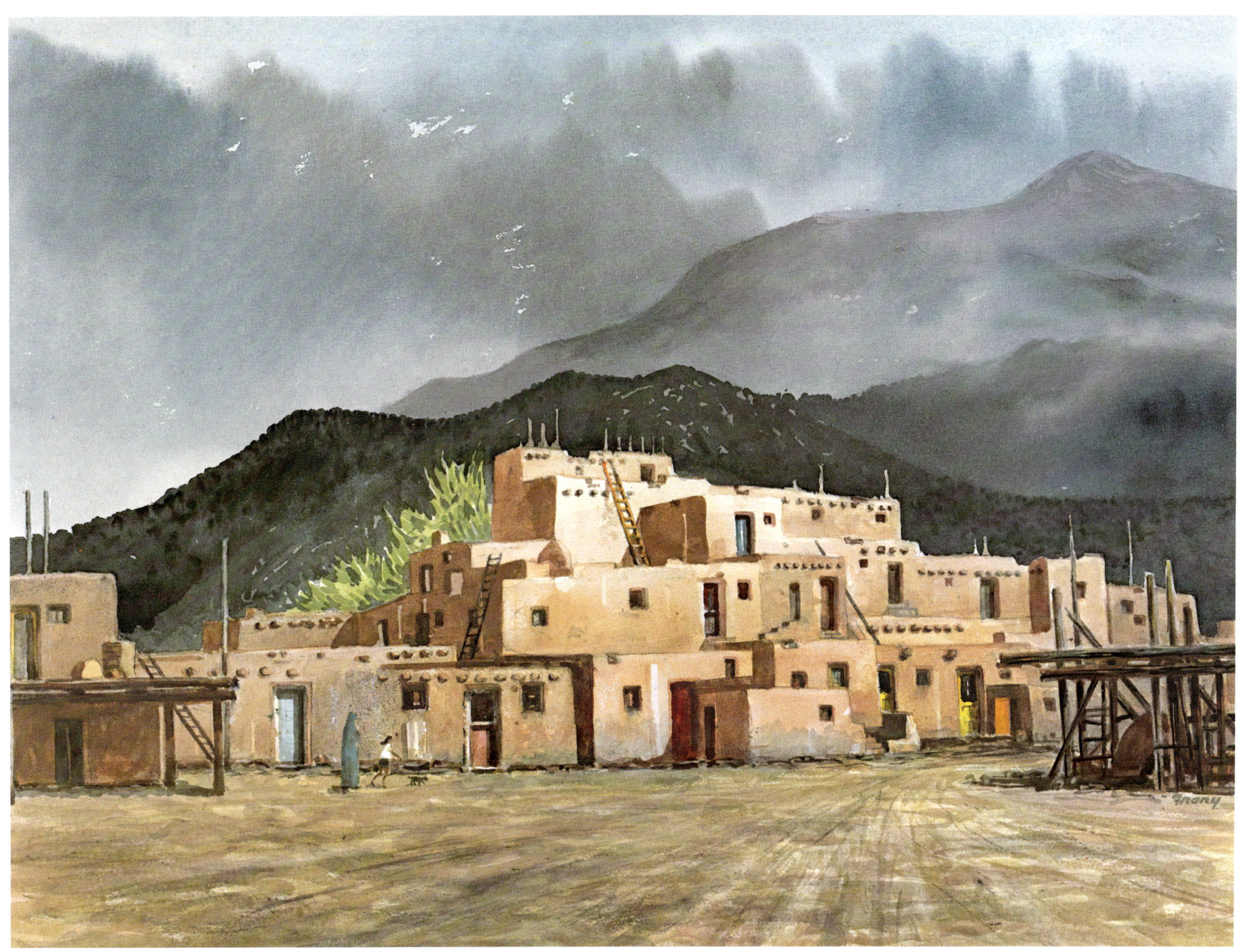

23. Picuris Pueblo

Picuris (pee-kuhr-rees´) is the smallest of the Tiwa pueblos, with only about two hundred residents. Nestled in the mountain valley of the Rio Pueblo between Taos and Santa Fe, it was founded between 1250 and 1300. The women pray to the clay gods before they go up to their secret place in the mountains to bring back clay for their ceramics. The clay they use contains mica, which produces a distinctive luster.

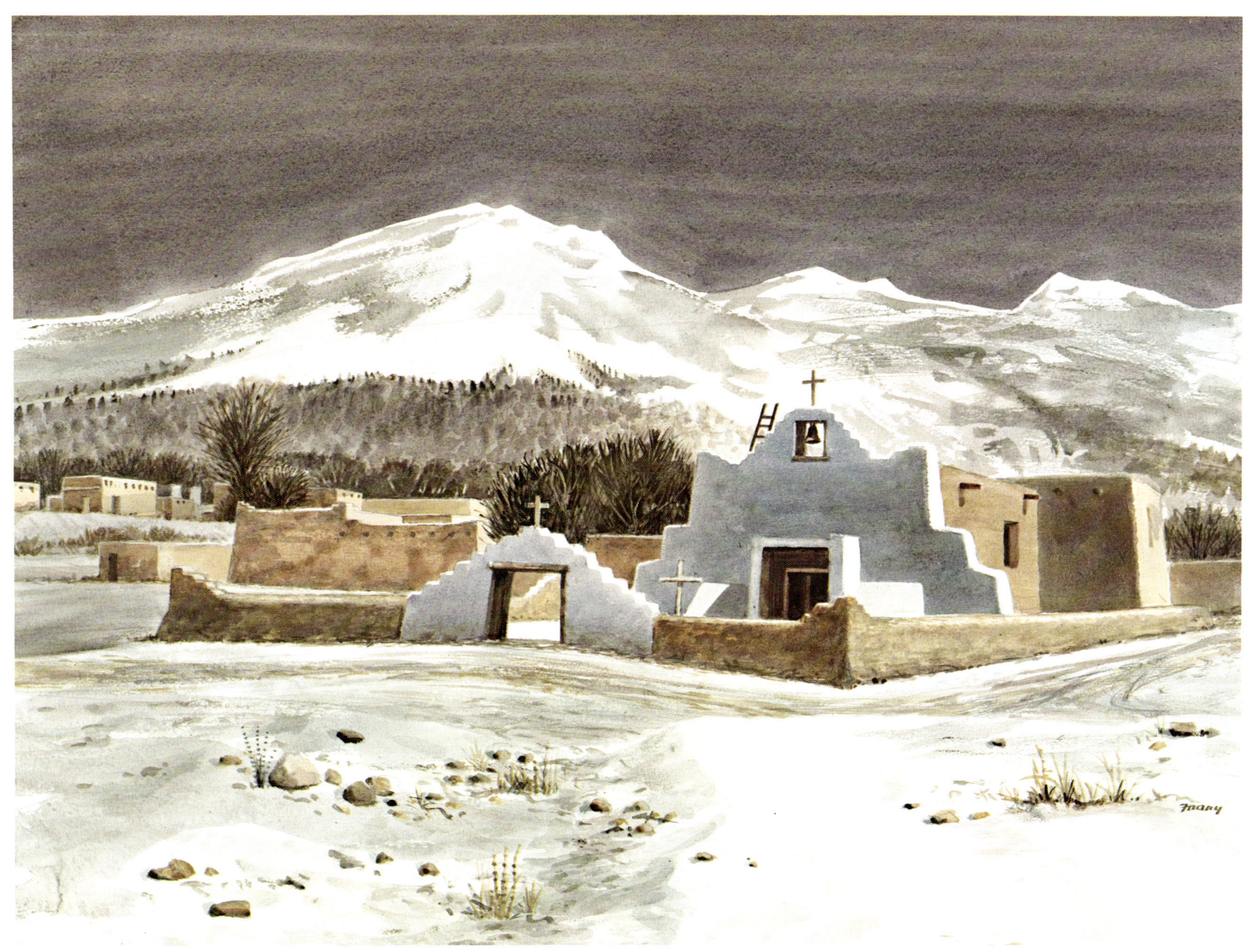

24. Festival at Puyé

Many pueblos have fiestas during which ceremonial dances are performed. The largest and most famous of the Rio Grande pueblo fiestas is the one at Santo Domingo. Here at the cliff dwelling ruins at Puyé (puh-yeh´), the Santa Clara pueblo has its fiestas. Because many other pueblos are also represented, there are a large variety of dances.

I struck up a conversation with a dignified, elderly Indian (who I expect was a chief) and asked him about the flag. He said that it symbolizes an everlasting universe, nature, and peace. I asked him why the rooms of the ruins were so small (they were about six feet square). He replied, "The people were smaller then." After a few seconds he added, "And the small rooms were easier to heat."

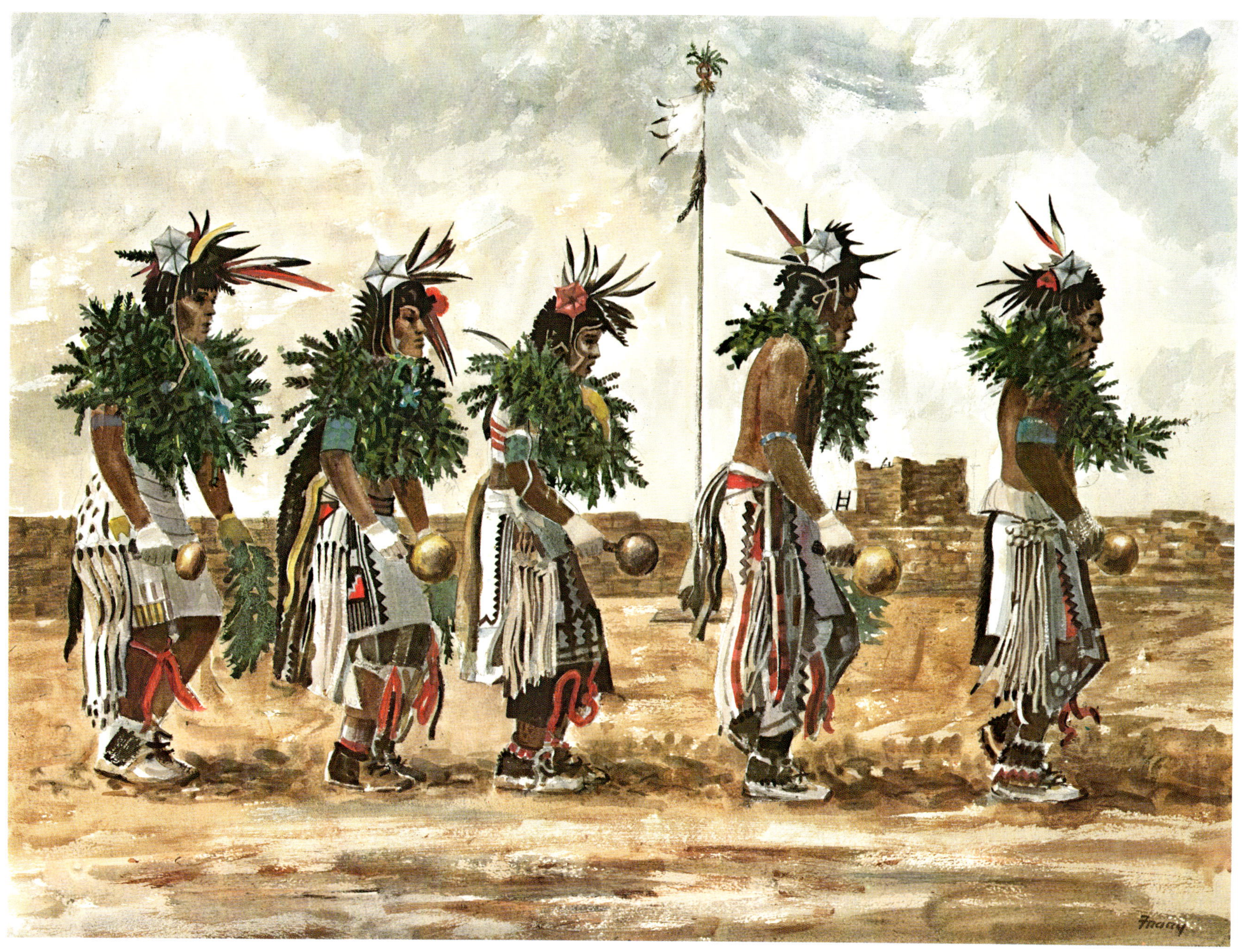

25. Church near Nambé

Nambé (nahm-bay´) is close to Santa Fe on the road to Taos. I was impressed with the monumental strength of this adobe structure and the sensitively designed white woodwork. Its dramatic placement on the hill and the texture of the ocotillo fence were also effective. I did not have to change anything in transposing this scene into a strong painting.

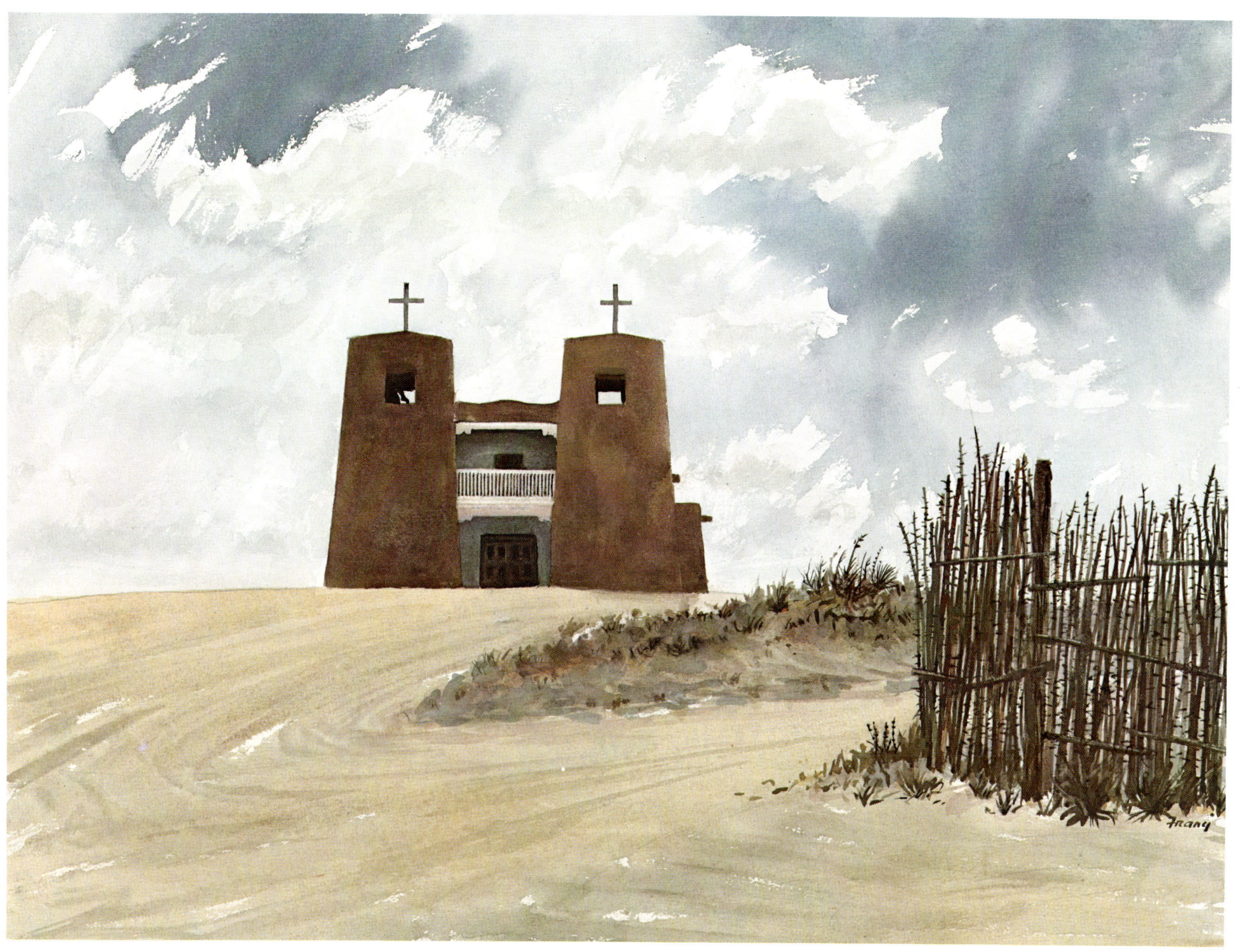

26. San Miguel Mission, Santa Fe

Authorities say that this church, begun about 1610, is the oldest still in use in the United States. Just to the left, up narrow De Vargas Street, is the oldest house, believed to be pre-Spanish. Santa Fe is considered by many to be one of the three or four most interesting towns in the United States. It was the center of Spanish settlement and is the oldest capital in America.

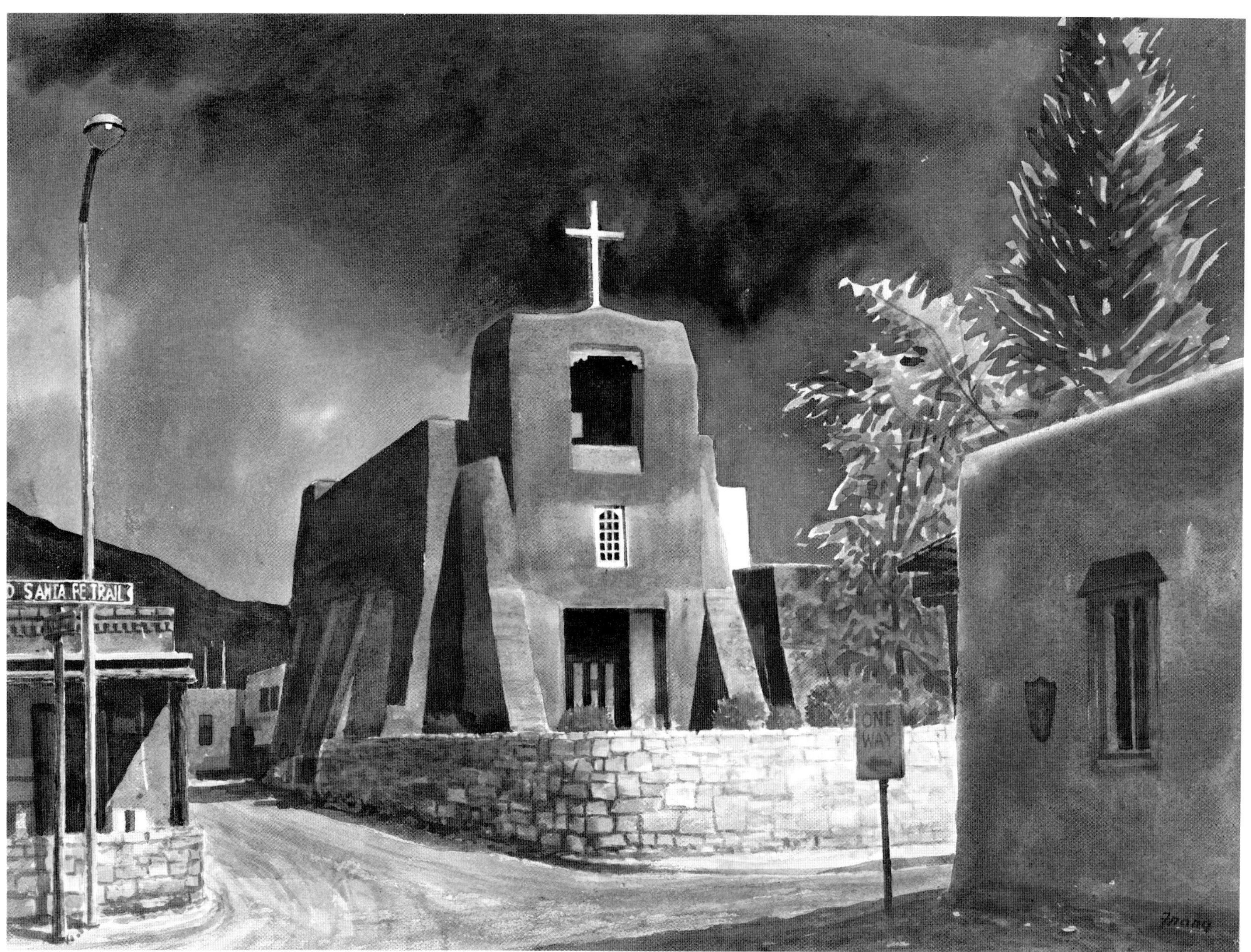
SANTA FE TRAIL
ONE WAY

27. Old Bridge near Los Alamos

I chose to do a painting of this bridge because of the repeated flat arches, the blue bushes in the foreground, and the feeling of loneliness that pervades a structure no longer used.

The nearby town of Los Alamos was taken over by the government in 1942 for nuclear research. It is a planned town—a quiet, clean, suburban community in magnificent surroundings, without a shred of the Indian-Spanish-Mexican tradition that makes Santa Fe and Taos so unusual.

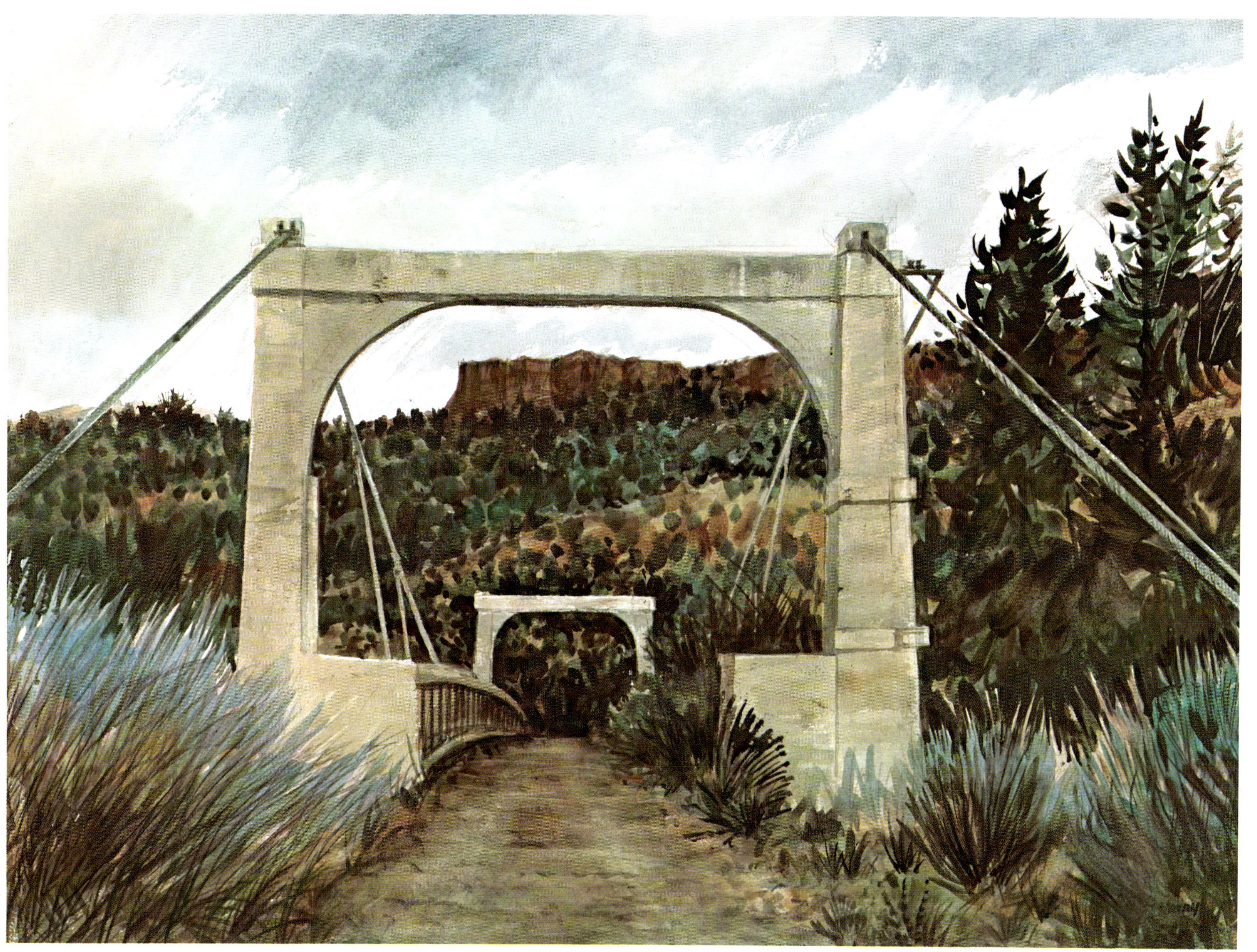

28. From a Kiva Painting at Kuaua

This is a watercolor interpretation of a reconstructed mural in a kiva at the Coronado State Monument near Bernalillo. Coronado, searching for the Seven Cities of Cibola, spent the winter of 1540 in the vicinity of Albuquerque. He claimed all the nearby Tiwa villages as part of Spain's Tiguex Province. Kuaua (kwa´-ah), Tiwa for "evergreen," is the northernmost village in the province. Kuaua was first settled about 1300.

The murals found here are some of the finest examples of prehistoric murals in the United States. Here at Kuaua the general public may go down into the kiva, usually off-limits, to see the murals. The kiva is accessible because Kuaua was abandoned hundreds of years ago.

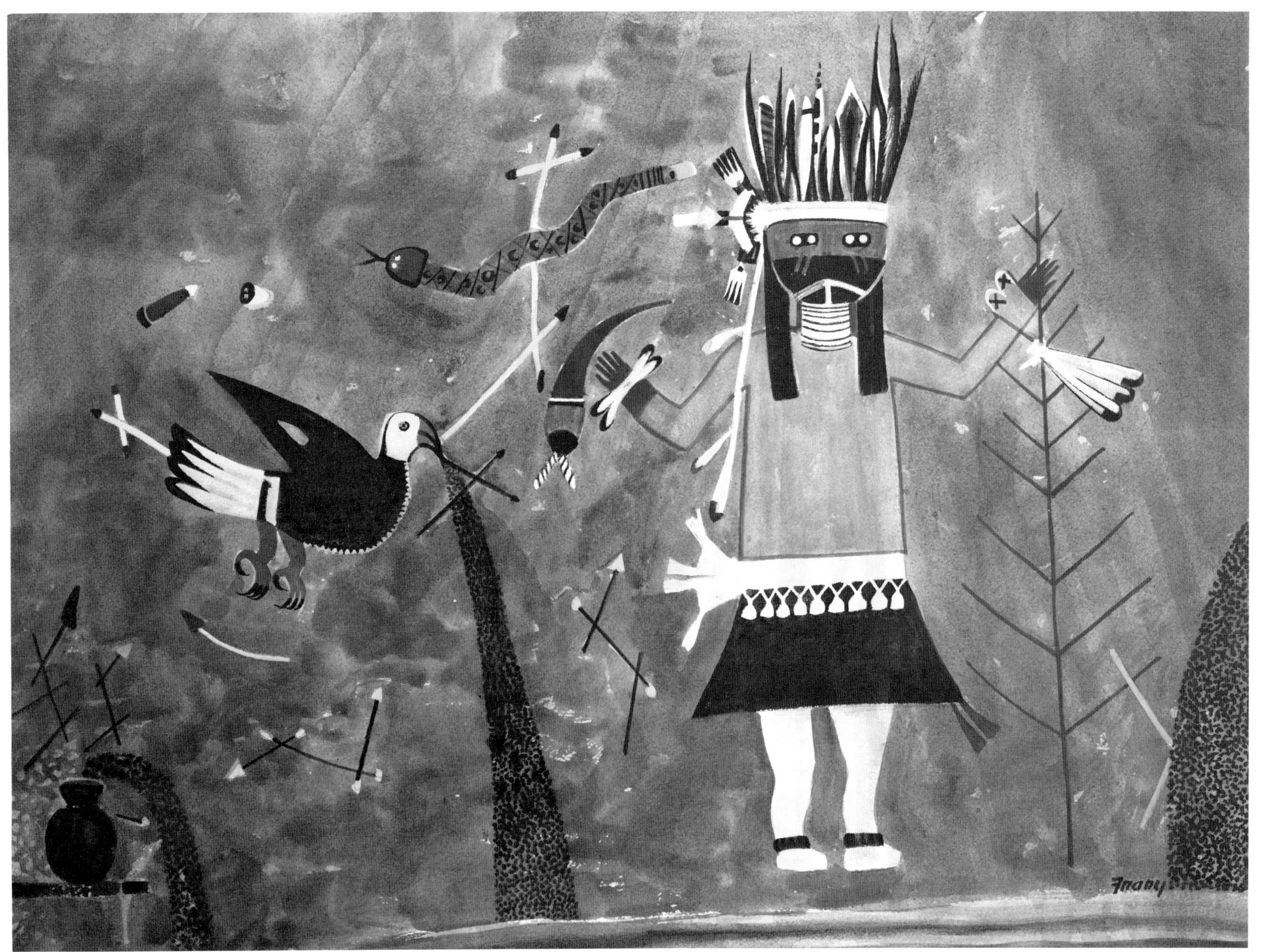

29. Dam at Isleta

Isleta (ees-lay´-tah), twelve miles south of Albuquerque, is the farthest south of the nineteen New Mexico pueblos. This pueblo, whose name means "little island," is the most populous of the Tiwa group, with twenty-eight hundred residents. Its mainstay is agriculture, and this dam assures the Isletans of enough water to irrigate their crops. The Indians have priority water rights because they have used the water productively for centuries. Downstream at this time, the riverbed was dry except for a few scattered ponds.

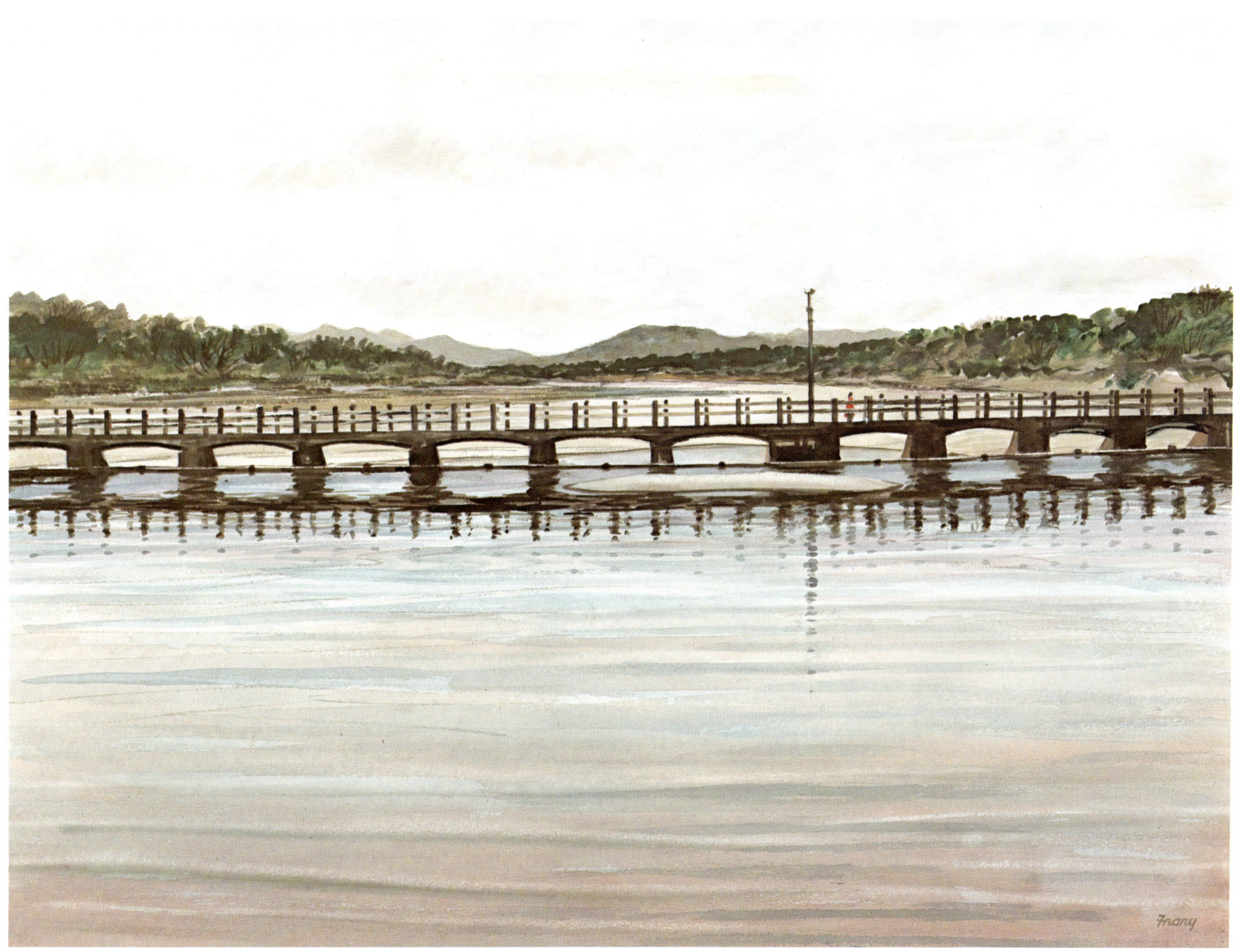

30. *White Sands*

The White Sands Missile Range lies on an unusual desert terrain. Actually, these dunes are not sand but small grains of crystallized gypsum that have been washed down into the valley by mountain streams.

After Po-pe, the amazingly efficient organizer of the successful Indian revolt of 1680, defeated the Spanish in northern New Mexico, the survivors were allowed to escape to El Paso down the Jornada del Muerto ("journey of the dead"), a valley just west of here.

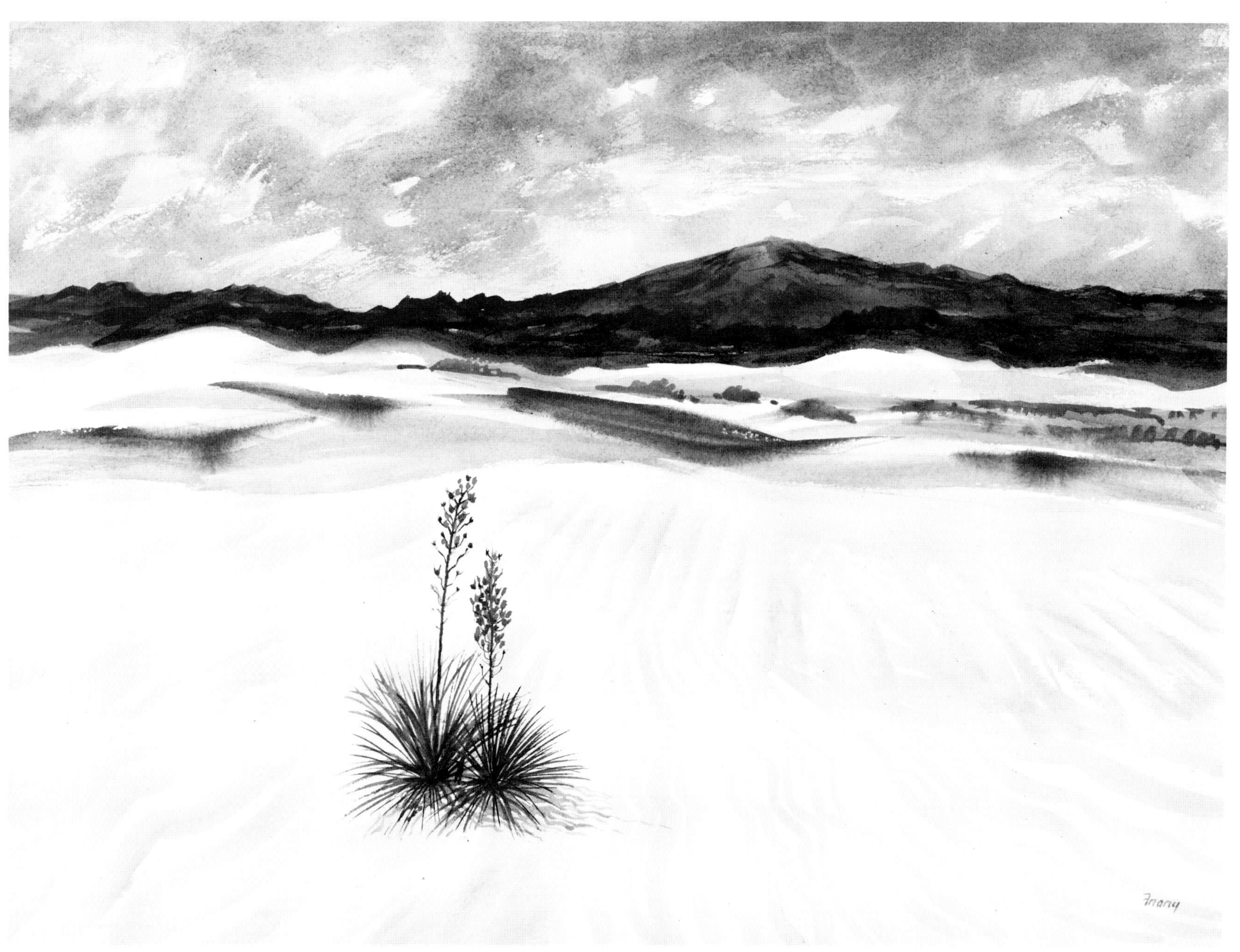

31. Elephant Butte Reservoir

Elephant Butte Dam is near the town named after the quiz show "Truth or Consequences." The reservoir thus formed is forty miles long and supplies water for the Rio Abajo ("lower river"). The holding basin for this reservoir is Caballo Lake, a sizable fifteen miles long. These two reservoirs attempt to control flooding downstream and at the same time distribute water to 300,000 acres, including the Rincon, Mesilla, El Paso, and Juárez valleys.

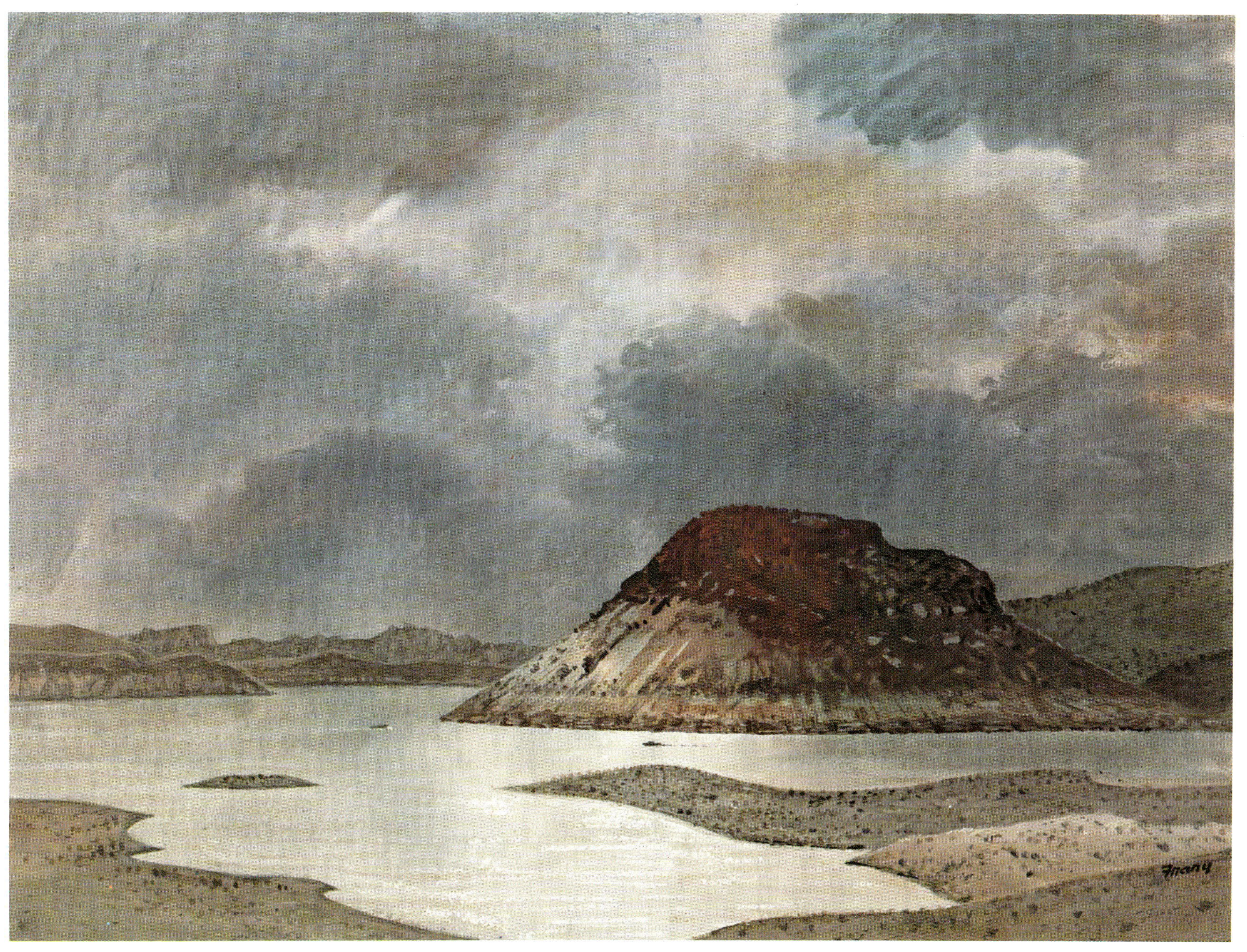

32. Mesilla–Las Cruces Area

The district south of Elephant Butte Reservoir and Caballo Lake is very productive. The Rio Grande again spreads out into canals and irrigates thousands of acres of cotton, lettuce, onions, chili, and other produce.

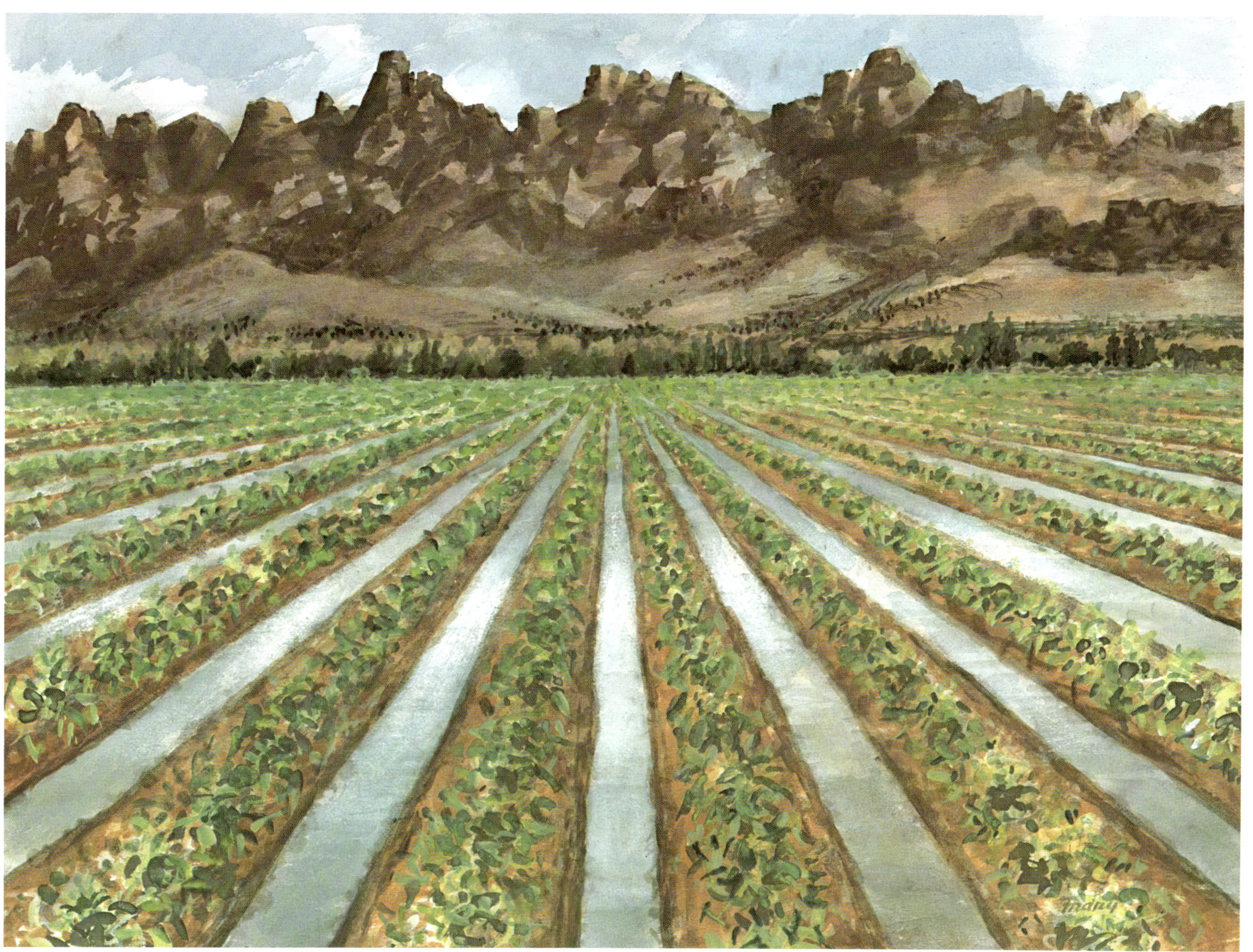

Part Three: The Texas-Mexico Rio Grande

The Texas-Mexico Rio Grande

As the Rio Grande leaves New Mexico it flows first south, then east through the pass around the bone-dry Franklin Mountains toward its final destination, the Gulf of Mexico, 1,248 miles downstream. It also begins its role as an international boundary between Texas and four Mexican states: Chihuahua, Coahuila, Nuevo León, and Tamaulipas. The river separates the large, industrial twin cities of El Paso (Texas) and Ciudad Juárez (Chihuahua).

This pass through the southern Rocky Mountains is famous historically: Cabeza de Vaca reportedly went through it in 1536, and Chamuscado led the first Spanish expedition through the pass to the north in 1581. Seventeen years later Juan de Oñate and four hundred men came through the pass on their way to Santa Fe and named it El Paso del Rio del Norte. De Oñate issued a proclamation known as La Toma, in which he took possession, for God and Spain, of all lands drained by the Rio Grande. Later the Mexican part of El Paso, south of the Rio Grande, was used as a base by such revolutionaries as Benito Juárez, Francisco Madero, and Pancho Villa, and the name was changed to Ciudad Juárez.

My memories of the El Paso area begin with having lunch at Anthony under the shade of a lonely tree on the west bank of the Rio Grande, followed by a short swim in the wide, muddy river. I remember admiring the curious Tibetan architecture of the University of Texas at El Paso and noticing that the Sun Bowl was indeed set in a natural bowl in the hills. The wind as well as the river sweeps through the pass. There is a fine view of bustling El Paso and sprawling Juárez from a high road called, I think, Scenic Drive. As the sun went down one summer day there was a haze over the area, and I saw blue hills in the background. The slanting rays of the sun hit the tall buildings in El Paso and a few in Juárez. The two towers of the Guadalupe Mission in downtown Juárez stood out, and I decided to do a painting of the church.

As I crossed the border the next day, I kept trying to find the river. All I could see were a few concrete channels with a trickle of water flowing in them. Across the border I was confronted with a bewildering mass of trucks, buses, cars, pedestrians, incomprehensible street signs, blind one-way narrow streets, and other hazards. Off the main streets, I sometimes saw evidence of abject poverty: shacks, dirt streets, water being hauled by buckets, and junkyards everywhere. Contrary to the prevalent "mañana" image of Mexico, however, most of the laborers were working at a fast pace in the hot sun, and the women were sweeping their dirt walks with authority. The brightly painted buildings and houses seemed to be a defiance of the people's difficult way of life. I didn't find poverty picturesque.

I did indeed paint the Guadalupe Mission, which was begun in 1659. I also liked the shadows on the massive church next door. Other old missions are still standing a few miles east of El Paso on the U.S. side of the border. The Ysleta, Socorro, and San Elizario missions were originally south of the Rio Grande before the huge flood of 1829 redirected it. Before the river was controlled, another more recent flood changed its course to flow south, then east. This cut the Chamisal district of Juárez off from Mexico, causing years of international dispute. President Kennedy settled the problem, and the area is now a Mexican park to honor friendship between Mexico and the United States.

El Paso (one-half million population) and Juárez (one million) combine to form the largest metropolitan area on the Rio Grande. Both of these cities are growing rapidly, and a water shortage threatens. Prior agreements reserve the river water for agriculture, so all of the Mexican share and 90 percent of the El Paso share of the river go to the farms.

Both cities depend on one underground formation, called the Hueco Bolson aquifer, for their supplies. This aquifer, formed in the distant past by the waters of the Rio Grande, is dropping rapidly. According to Richard Marston, a hydrologist at the University of Texas at El Paso, even if this dry area received more than its yearly average of eight inches of rainfall, the aquifer would not benefit: the soil over the recharge zone is impermeable, and the rainfall runs off or evaporates.

To alleviate this problem, El Paso is trying to supplement its supplies by importing water from New Mexico to the northwest, which is over the large Mesilla Bolson aquifer. The difficulty in this solution is that New Mexico laws prohibit the export of water. This, then, is a serious problem and calls for adequate planning.

The pass is heavily populated because in 1881, four railroad lines connected at this spot. Consequently, the population expanded rapidly, embracing not only serious settlers—farmers and businessmen—but also serious revolutionaries—smugglers and gunslingers. At one time El Paso had a reputation as the "sin center" of the Southwest. Today it seems to be a rather conservative, rapidly growing "sun city" with banking, clothing, and copper its main industries. The memory I have of leaving El Paso in my locally purchased Tony Lama boots is the two-pound steak I had at the Indian Cliffs Ranch, about thirty miles to the east.

As the now-depleted Rio Grande passes through the El Paso–Juárez Valley, it continues to irrigate a few farms along the way; by the Fort Hancock and Fort Quitman areas, however, the last of the water that started at Stony Pass is used up. The changeable Rio Grande is bone-dry. As Will Rogers put it, the Rio Grande is "the first river I've seen that needs irrigating."

The river has ventured about seven hundred miles from its source and irrigated one million acres. For the next one hundred forty miles, as the crow flies, the old riverbed runs through a dry desert valley. The highway leaves the riverbed, with only a few primitive roads and no inhabitants on either side for many miles. I had a feeling of being closed in and could easily understand why nobody lives here.

Throughout the dry expanses of sand I saw cactus, birds, reptiles, insects, and other creatures that survive in this stark, blistering furnace. It occurred to me that this region is the exact opposite of the snow-capped peaks of the great San Juan Mountains. Survival, however, is just as trying. In each case, the animals, insects, and plants have specialized characteristics that enable them to live and reproduce in an extremely hostile environment.

In 1980 the river bottom at Candelaria was so full of silt that it was higher than the surrounding land; in other places, salt cedars and desert willows masked the river bottom. Because a 1970 treaty specifies the middle of the river as the boundary between Mexico and the United States, both governments wanted to define the boundary. In order to find the river, the International Water Boundary Commission had to use early aerial maps to determine the old channel. Subsequently, in the summer of 1980, a trench six feet deep and fifty-six feet wide was dug through the dry sand and boulders to help define this isolated section of the border. This part of the river is another extreme of the unique Rio Grande.

At Presidio (Texas) and Ojinaga (Chihuahua), the Río Conchos comes surging out of the Chihuahuan Desert mountains to become the Rio Grande's second stage. Perhaps from this point on, the Rio Grande should more aptly be named the Río Bravo del Norte, as the Mexican maps show. There is a small, fertile valley here known as La Junta de los Rios. Evidence indicates that some of the first inhabitants of what is now Texas lived in this area about twelve thousand years ago.

Nearby, old Fort Leaton has been reconstructed with adobe made on the spot. Ben Leaton, a desperado, and three other men deserted during the Mexican War and lived as bandits in the ruins of this early eighteenth-century mission, which they called Fort Leaton. The story goes that Leaton, in order to increase his profits in smuggling and trading, gave a party for about forty local Indians and Mexicans, who proceeded to drink a great deal. The next day Leaton found that about forty of his horses and some cattle were missing. After a couple of months, he invited everybody back for another bash. During the height of the party, Leaton opened a window onto the patio and killed all his guests with a cannon full of shot, nails, and scrap metal. This was frontier life in the "bloody bend," where smuggling and banditry were the rule, and retaliation was sometimes swift and terrible.

Downstream from Presidio the River Road (El Camino del Río) hugs the banks of the Rio Grande. This is rugged country, sometimes referred to as the badlands of Texas. I saw massive, layered limestone cliffs with dark basalt ridges and strange, haunting vertical shapes of tuff, which is hardened volcanic ash. Every plant around here seems to have thorns. In this northern edge of the Chihuahuan Desert the Rio Grande seems to provide the only cool, welcome change from the awesome austerity of the region. The River Road runs for fifty miles along the bank of the river, and at Lajitas ("flat rocks") the road turns away from the river toward the famous old mining ghost town of Terlingua.

Lajitas, once a U.S. cavalry outpost, was established to protect the settlers from Pancho Villa and other bandidos. It was built at the San Carlos crossing, where the Comanche and Apache Indians rode the Comanche war trail across the ford to invade Mexico. Houston industrialist Walter Mischer has financed extensive developments in the style of the 1890s and has thoughtfully preserved some of the original buildings. Today, Lajitas has an impressive new museum to preserve its heritage. While I was in town painting the Old Trading Post, I was visited by a friendly goat who liked to have his picture taken and drink beer.

Lajitas is close to the western end of the unique Big Bend National Park, 1,100 square miles of wildly weird wilderness. Three awe-inspiring canyons have been carved through three mountain ranges by the Rio Grande, which forms 107 miles of the park boundary. Lajitas is the put-in point for boating Santa Elena Canyon, the first and most dangerous of the canyons for river runners. This canyon cuts through the seemingly impenetrable Mesa de Anguila, with sheer walls fifteen hundred feet high. A well-known feature of this canyon is the Rock Slide, with room-sized boulders piled two hundred feet high. The river leaves the canyon just as abruptly as it enters, then flows through about fifty miles of open desert to the next challenge, Mariscal Canyon.

The Mariscal is located at the southernmost extreme of the Big Bend. It is a beautiful canyon and the deepest in the park, with vertical walls seventeen hundred feet high. The Mariscal has very primitive roads to the put-in point at Talley. On the way to canoe and paint Mariscal, I was driving a rented motor home; because of the rolling, twisting dirt road, the drive shaft bushing broke. Luckily for me, the driver of the next vehicle in the group crawled under my R.V. in the hot sand and miraculously repaired it. My benefactor was the director of education of the Chihuahuan Desert Research Institute of Alpine (Texas), an organization renowned for its continuing research on and promotion of this breathtakingly diverse and scientifically significant region.

The Mariscal has its own challenges. The Tight Squeeze swamped six out of twelve canoes in our party. Unless the water is high, however, there are not many dangerous rapids. As I drifted with the current in these canyons, I felt an eerie silence. But when I rounded the bend and heard a distant rumble from the next rapids, my reverie changed to suspense. I was impressed by the grandeur of the cliffs and the constantly changing light and dark. By moonlight the place evokes a feeling of mystery. I painted the Break in the middle of the canyon, which marks a trail of Comanche raiders who used to ride deep into Mexico every September during the full moon, which they called the Mexican Moon, to bring back horses and cattle. (The Mexicans called it the Comanche Moon.) On the Mexican side of the Break, I saw Indian petroglyphs and a candelilla wax camp. Candelilla is a cactus from which a high-quality wax is produced.

At the east end of the Big Bend Park is Boquillas Canyon, the longest (twenty-five miles) and most serene of the three. It cuts directly through the Sierra del Carmen range.

The Big Bend canyons are much different from the Rio Grande Gorge canyons: first of all, their walls are more perpendicular. Also, the mountains seem to rise on either side of the Rio Grande in the Big Bend area, whereas the river cuts down into the Taos Plateau to form the gorge. In the Big Bend the sheer walls are not much wider at the top than at the bottom and are two to three times higher than in the gorge.

A question that puzzles me is, How did the river cut through these three canyons? The Rio Grande travels generally from west to east through three mountain ranges that run north to south. Between each mountain range lie forty or more miles of flat desert land, through which the river meanders until it decides to slice through another mountain range to the east.

The three canyons form a V-shape that surrounds the Chisos Mountains. The Chisos rise to almost eight thousand feet and form a biological island in the midst of a desert. The name *chisos,* which means "ghosts," "spirits," or "enchantment," is very appropriate for this area. There are many legends about the devil, the Apache chief Alsate's ghost, the treasure of the Lost Mine, and others. I had heard about the mysterious Marfa lights, and while teaching one summer at Sul Ross University in Alpine, I drove six or seven times to the runway of an abandoned airport near Marfa. Every night I saw up to six or eight distinct lights toward the south go on for a few minutes and then go off. There was no moon, and neither roads nor habitation lay in that direction. Some who have studied the lights claim to have seen them suddenly swoop together to form a large mass of light. They were first noted by diaries of pioneers in the 1850s. I have yet to hear a reasonable explanation for these lights.

It is appropriate that a giant crocodile-like reptile fifty feet long is known to have lived in this lost world. In 1971, fossil bones of the pterosaur, the most spectacular flying creature ever to have evolved, were found in the Big Bend. Its wing spread was estimated to have been fifty-one feet.

An early Spaniard who tried to capture the true spirit of the Big Bend composed this memorable description:

You go south from Fort Davis,
Where the rainbow waits for the rain,
Where the river is kept in a stone box
And the water runs uphill,
And the mountains tower into the sky.
Except at night,
When they disappear to visit other mountains.

The Big Bend is truly a vast, complex, and mysterious area. It is comparatively well known and well traveled, however, in relation to the Rio Grande's course northeast after it leaves the park. The Lower Canyons of the Rio Grande, which stretch for 191 miles, were aptly named Despoblado by the Spaniards, meaning "unpopulated" or, more mysteriously, "the place where nobody goes," "no man's land." When you commit yourself to a raft or a canoe at the put-in at La Linda (Mexico), there is no turning back. When I canoed it with a group from the University of Texas Athletic Department the water was high, and we took six days to get to Dudley's Landing, near Dryden. My canoe swamped about three times every day, most dangerously when it hung up on a boulder at Burro Bluff rapids. I made it to the shore, and with help from another canoeing party we managed to rescue the canoe. We damaged only our pride—the two men who swung hand-over-hand on a rope to dislodge my canoe were Aggies from Texas A&M. Everything was tied down and in plastic bags, so my painting equipment and duffle bag stayed relatively dry. There were no serious casualties on the trip—just ten tired river runners and five severely dented and patched canoes at the end.

The river, after passing through treeless desert country, glides by Roy Bean's famous "law west of the Pecos" saloon-courthouse at Langtry. It is then reinforced by the large Pecos River and the Devil's River entering from the north to form the eighty-thousand-acre Amistad Reservoir. I was surprised by the lack of any plants or trees along the shoreline. The twin cities of Del Rio and Ciudad Acuña (about nine hundred fifty feet above sea level) border both the Edwards Plateau and the Texas Hill Country. For the first time since near Fort Quitman, I saw water used for irrigation.

Downstream at Eagle Pass (Texas) and Piedras Negras (Coahuila), the Rio Grande has 727 feet left to descend. This is the port of entry onto the Constitution Highway to Mexico City via Saltillo and San Luis Potosí. From here southeast to Laredo–Nuevo Laredo, the river cuts through large ranches with very few access roads. There are mesquite, chaparral, and huge prickly pear or nopal, with joints bigger than tennis racquets. Nuevo Laredo marks the north end of the Pan American Highway, making Laredo the most important U.S. gateway to Mexico for rail and highway traffic. Laredo's population is about 85,000, and Nuevo Laredo's is about 205,000. The larger population of the Mexican twin city reflects a pattern common to other twin cities along the border.

This brings up a very interesting historical footnote. In 1750 José de Escandón, Spain's ablest colonizer, organized seven columns of over one hundred troops each. He had them converge to rendezvous at the mouth of the Rio Grande in order to select good sites for cities. In addition to the string of Rio Grande cities such as Laredo, de Escandón chose two northeastern sites: one was present-day Goliad, and the other was Villa de Vedoya, or present-day Corpus Christi. For whatever reason (some sources say that the Spanish government refused to advance 5,000 pesos), the twenty-five families designated for each of these two locations ended up south of the river, in northeastern Mexico. If José de Escandón's plans had materialized, by the early 1800s the Spanish (later Mexican) culture would have dominated south Texas instead of the Anglo influence of Stephen Austin's colonizers. There probably would have been neither a defense of the Alamo nor the battle ending in Santa Anna's defeat. Mexico might have settled not only Texas but also the western states, leaving the United States confined to the eastern states. Mexico would then have been the dominant country on the continent.

José de Escandón, knighted by the Spanish king, was very successful south of the border and settled over six thousand citizens in twenty-three towns. This northward colonial drive is the basic reason for the large population in northeastern Mexico today and explains why the Mexican border towns are much bigger than their U.S. counterparts.

Thirty-three miles beyond Laredo, I "discovered" the architecturally interesting old town of San Ygnacio. This small, quiet town is near the north end of Falcon Lake. Falcon Dam backs up three million acre-feet of water to make this reservoir the largest on the river. The lake is also fed by the Mexican Río Salado and Río Sabinas. The water is used to irrigate the Rio Grande Valley of Texas, one of the richest river deltas in the world. I found that the last part of the Rio Grande from Laredo to the Gulf of Mexico is roughly divided into two separate ecological systems. South and east from Laredo through Rio Grande City to a few miles west of Mission, the rolling, dry desert plains are covered with mesquite and prickly pear. Gradually the rolling hills disappear. The flat land brings about a complete transformation: canals begin to irrigate almost a million acres of citrus and other crops on both sides of the border. It seems cooler, wetter, and less dusty from Mission to the east. Near Mission in the Santa Ana National Wildlife Refuge, I did a painting of the moss-covered national champion ebony tree. I tried to paint a *chachalaca*, a turkey-sized bird found only in south Texas, but none would hold still. I painted a large dam at Mission several times.

The river is larger here. In the early 1800s paddle-wheelers used to carry cargo and passengers as far upriver as Rio Grande City and Roma–Los Saenz. Captain Richard King operated one of the riverboats and subsequently developed the great King Ranch to the north.

There are many toll bridges and some free border crossings between Falcon Lake and the Gulf of Mexico. I enjoyed exploring the minor crossings in this area. The one at Rio Grande City leads to Camargo, one of my favorite little Mexican towns, where I did a painting of the newly painted church. The most unusual crossing, however, is at Los Ebanos ("the ebonies"), which boasts a hand-pulled ferry—the only one on the U.S. border. After crossing and going a mile on a dirt road, I came to a small, nontourist, friendly town called Diaz Ordaz. Two neatly uniformed schoolchildren and I had a conversation while I was painting a local scene.

The entire lower Rio Grande Valley is growing rapidly. Thousands flock here for the winter, and there are many hospitals, rest homes, and other fine facilities for retired people. Palms, bougainvillaea, poinsettias, and citrus trees are surrounded by orange and grapefruit groves, and irrigated vegetable and cotton fields flourish. All of this makes the valley attractive to northerners.

The three largest cities on the U.S. side of the border are McAllen, Harlingen, and Brownsville; Reynosa and Matamoros are the largest Mexican towns. Brownsville is an international seaport and claims to be the home port of the nation's largest shrimp fleet. It is more southerly than any continental American city except Key West. Its relatively cool breezes from the Gulf and the palm, papaya, and banana trees that line its streets make clear its tropical nature. Brownsville's sister city, Matamoros, has more than twice the population of Brownsville. It boasts a rich and colorful history, and today its diversified industry makes it one of Mexico's wealthiest towns.

The last part of the Rio Grande's voyage is full of loops and curves—it travels a hundred miles to go thirty miles to the coast.

It seems to be reluctant to complete its long journey. In its wanderings the river sometimes loops back on itself, and *resacas*, sometimes called ox-bow or horseshoe lakes, are formed. Many of these lakes, being the old course of the river, are long and narrow, usually with lush vegetation on their banks. The Rio Grande is now a tropical river, as Piñeda realized in 1519 when he sailed his galleons upstream and named it Río de las Palmas. The Great River slowly meanders down the last few miles and, observed by a few fishermen at lonely Boca Chica, delivers its surprisingly clear water into the Gulf of Mexico. And from there perhaps some of it is borne on high winds back to Stony Pass.

33. Guadalupe Mission–Ciudad Juárez

This is the most important historic landmark in the El Paso–Juárez area. The large church, begun in 1659, dominates the other buildings in downtown Juárez and is considered to be architecturally one of the finest in Mexico. Juárez has about twice the population of its twin city, El Paso, and the plaza in front of the church and nearby side streets must be one of the busiest places in Mexico.

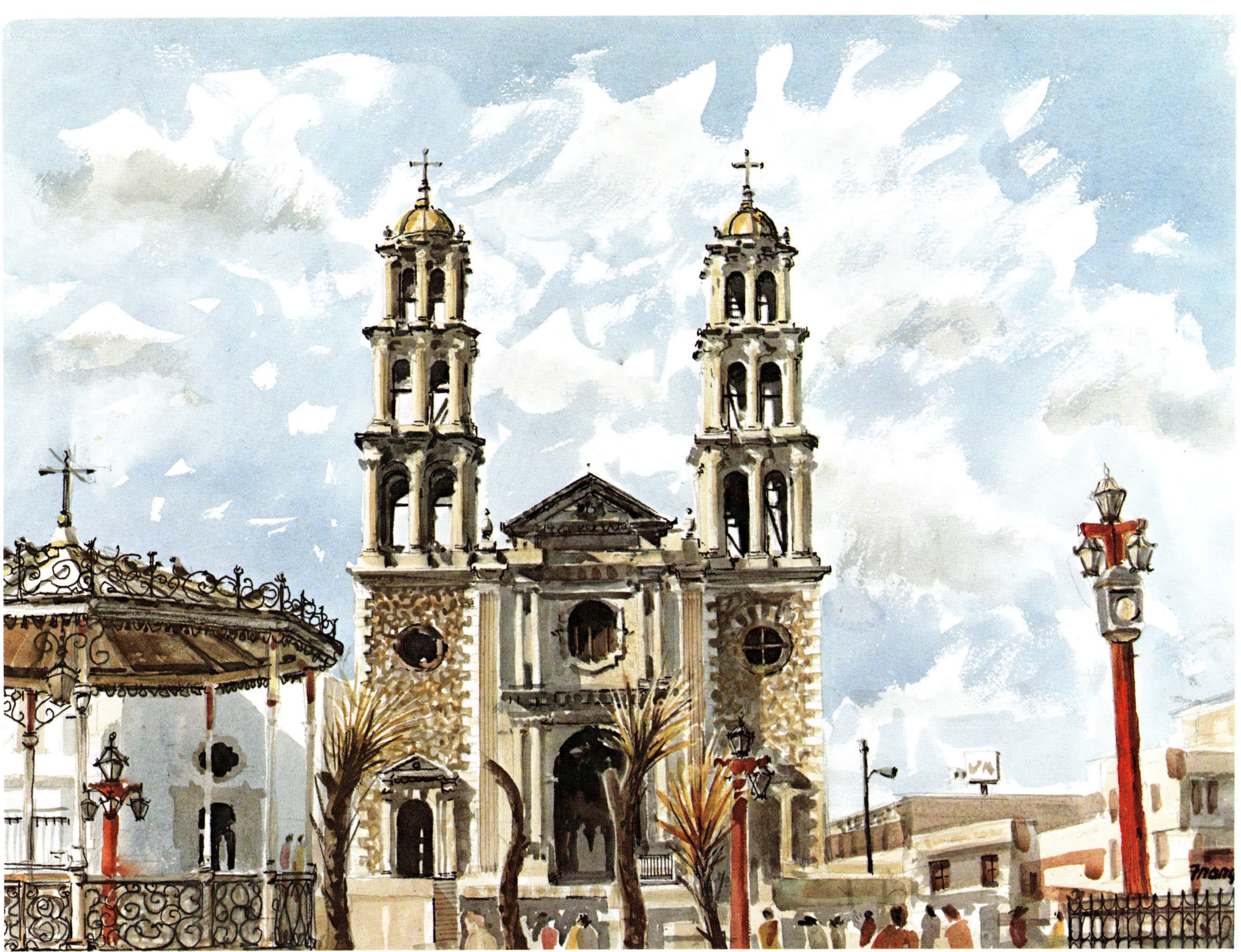

34. Cathedral of Our Lady of Guadalupe

Next door to the larger Guadalupe Mission is the strikingly simple Cathedral of Our Lady of Guadalupe. It seems strange to me that this smaller church should be named the cathedral. I was impressed by the strong geometric look and the shadows that identify its form.

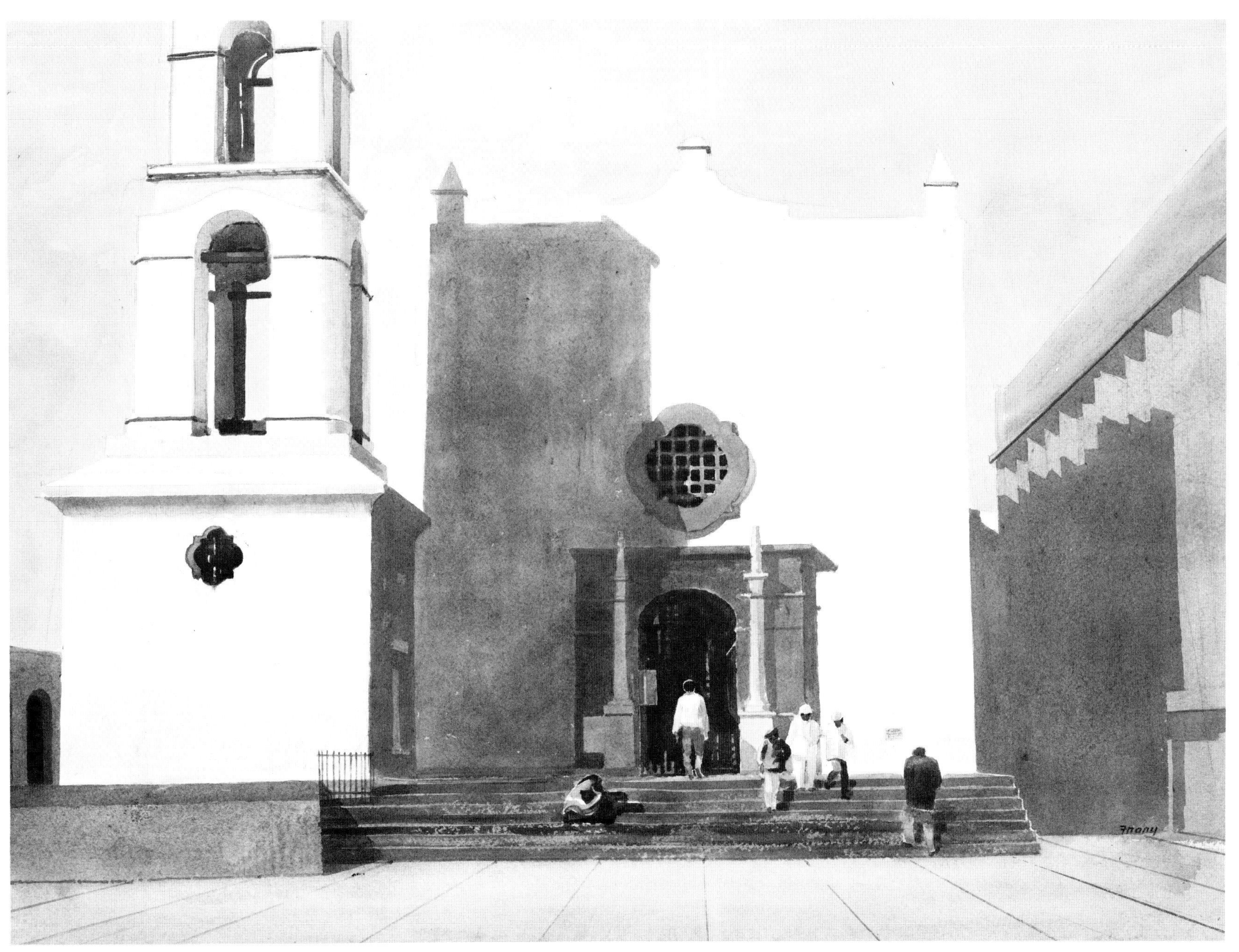

35. *Fort Leaton*

Ben Leaton, along with three other deserters from the U.S. Army during the Mexican War, lived as bandits near Presidio. They took over the ruins of this early eighteenth-century mission and called it Fort Leaton. There are many stories of smugglers, thieves, and killers that reflect the precariousness of frontier life in the "bloody bend." This very large adobe structure has been rebuilt with mud and straw bricks made on the premises and is still standing today. In some of the large storage rooms the ceilings and mud roofs, more than fifteen feet high, are supported by "columns" or pylons of adobe eight feet thick in order to shorten the length of the scarce ceiling log beams.

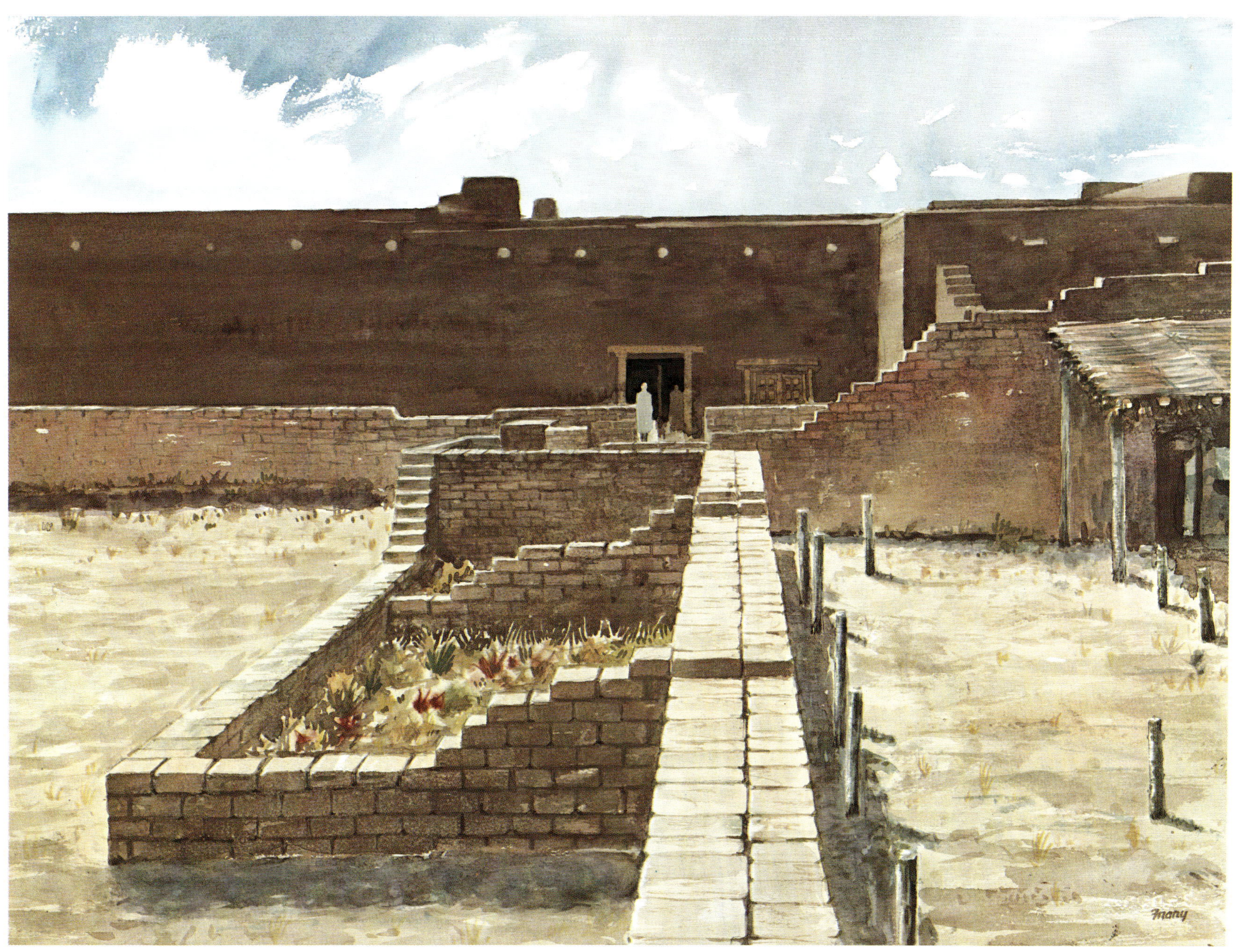

36. Morning Light, Lajitas

Lajitas and the ghost town of Terlingua are the two most widely known settlements between Presidio and the Big Bend. Lajitas used to be an outpost for the U.S. cavalry and was established to protect the settlers. It was built at the San Carlos crossing, one of the war trails of the Comanche and Apache Indians. The Indians used to cross here in large numbers every September and raid northern Mexico, bringing back up to ten thousand horses a year. The Mexicans became accomplished in protecting themselves during September, the month they called the Comanche Moon.

I liked the sparkle of morning light falling on Clay Henry, the beer-drinking goat, and his two friends.

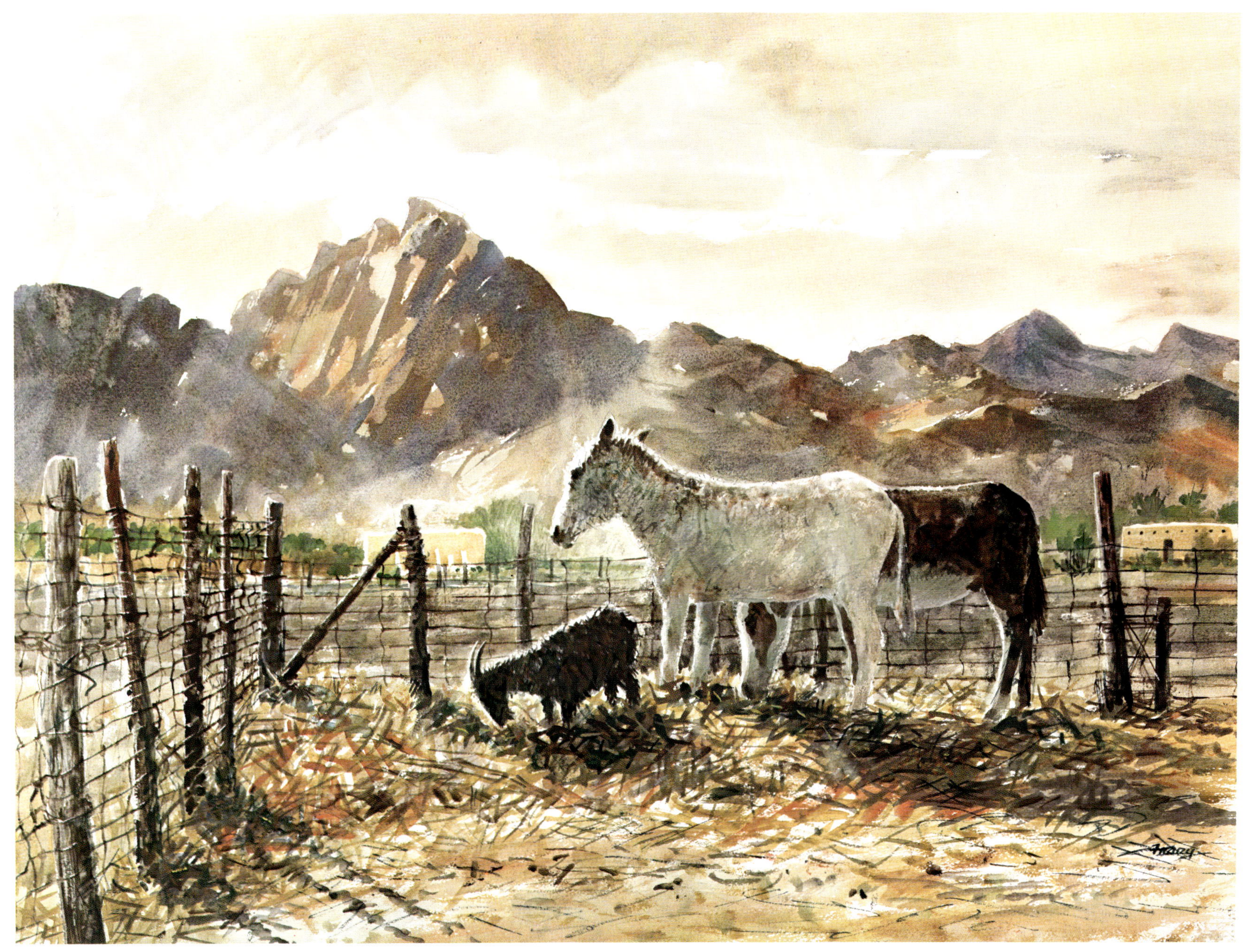

37. Santa Elena Canyon

After putting in at Lajitas, the river runner enters a narrow vertical slit in the seemingly impenetrable Mesa de Anguila. Suddenly the desert glare is extinguished by the dark and silent depths of gigantic, perpendicular canyon walls. After navigating the Rock Slide and other especially hazardous passages, the boater leaves the canyon as abruptly as he entered it. Upon leaving the canyon at Costollon, the river runs generally southeast through about fifty miles of open desert to the next challenge, the Mariscal.

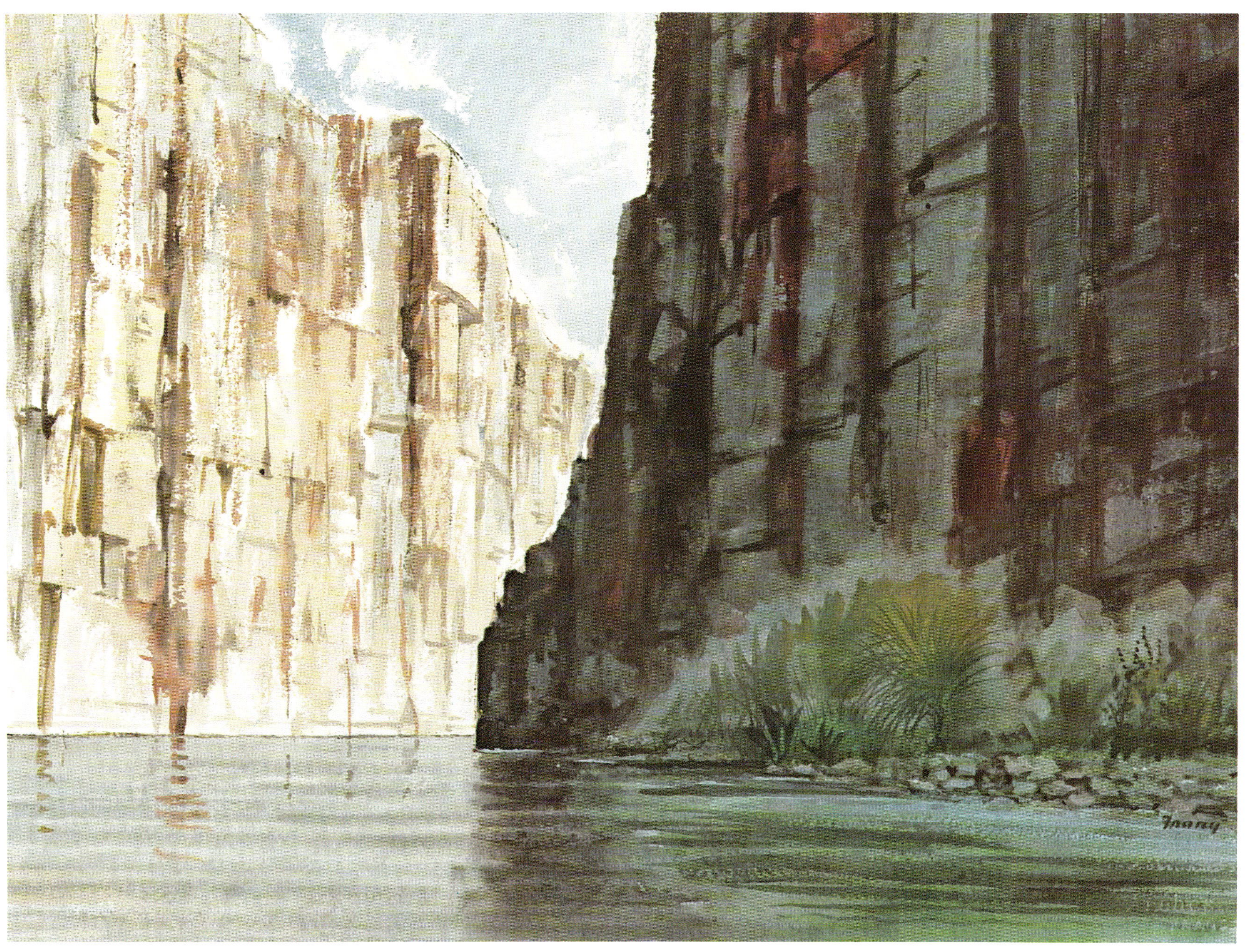

38. Solis

After a leisurely two days passing through the Mariscal Canyon, we took the canoes out of the Rio Grande here at Solis. This is a desolate spot, the southernmost part of the Big Bend.

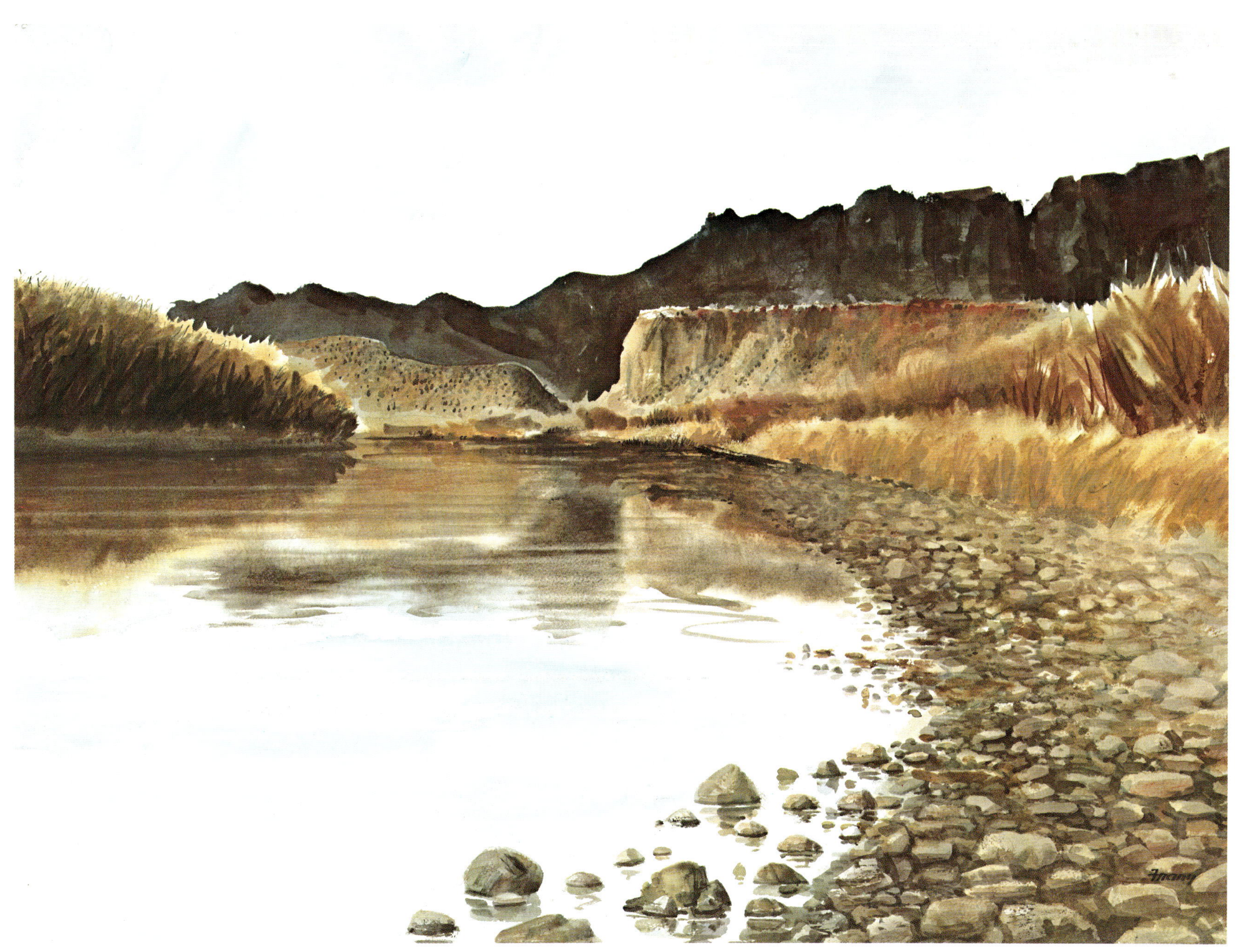

39. Wax Workers

After we arrived at Solis two candelilla wax workers crossed the river to say hello. We gave them some cans of sardines and other food that we had left over. Candelilla is a type of pencil-thin cactus that workers first tie in bundles, then boil by the side of the river. The fine-quality wax is used for many purposes. From here the river changes direction and flows northeast across a sandy stretch of about forty miles to face its third challenge, the Sierra del Carmen range and Boquillas Canyon.

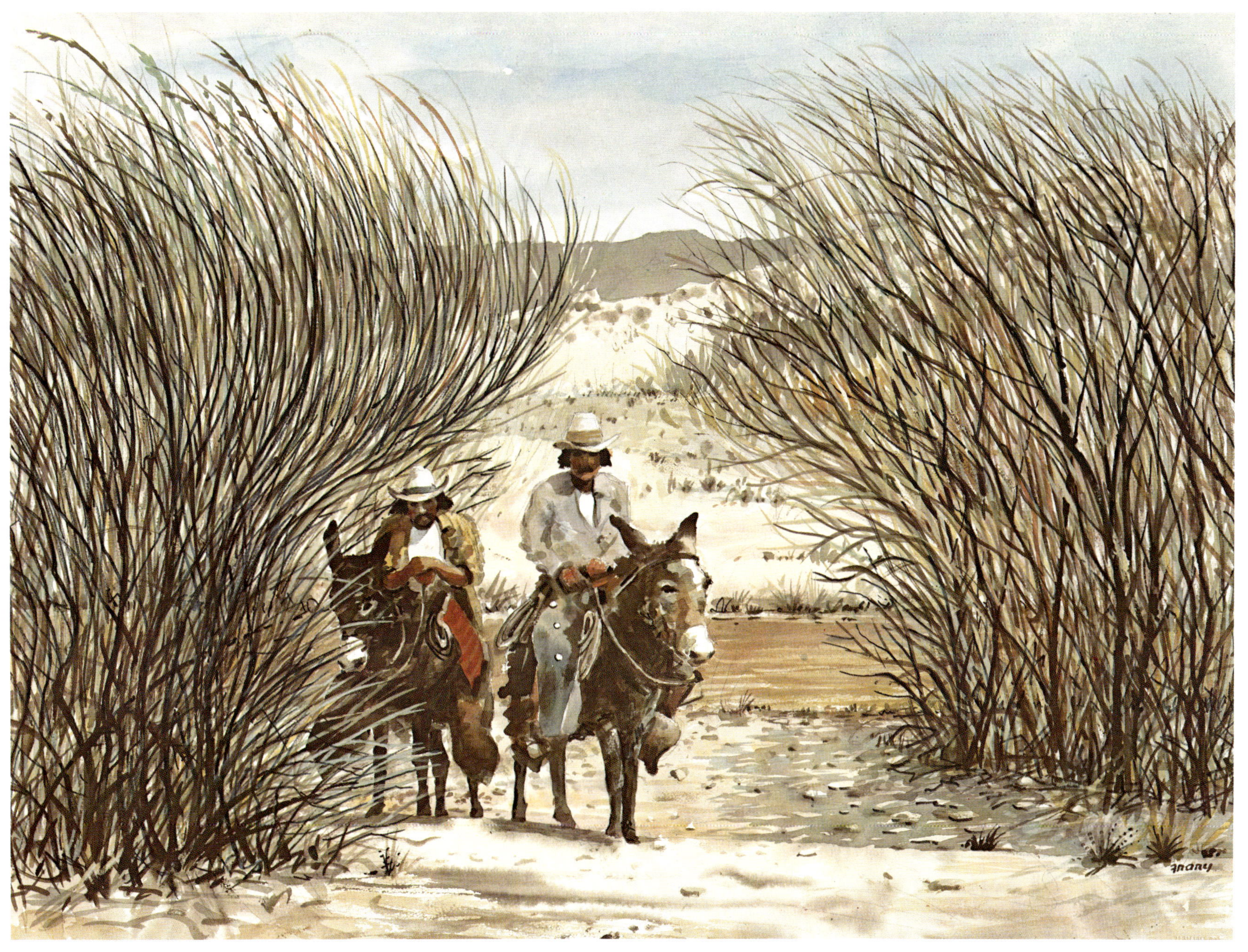

40. White Water, Lower Canyons

The Lower Canyons of the Rio Grande extend for eighty-five miles from La Linda (Mexico), just east of Big Bend National Park, to Dryden Crossing, thirty-five miles west of Langtry. Untouched wilderness, canyon walls rising fifteen hundred feet, hot springs, side canyons with clear pools, and grade four rapids are some of the many attractions. The Lower Canyons area was designated "wild and scenic" by Congress in 1978. When I canoed the Lower Canyons the water was high, and every canoe, except that of our leader, swamped from two to five times each day.

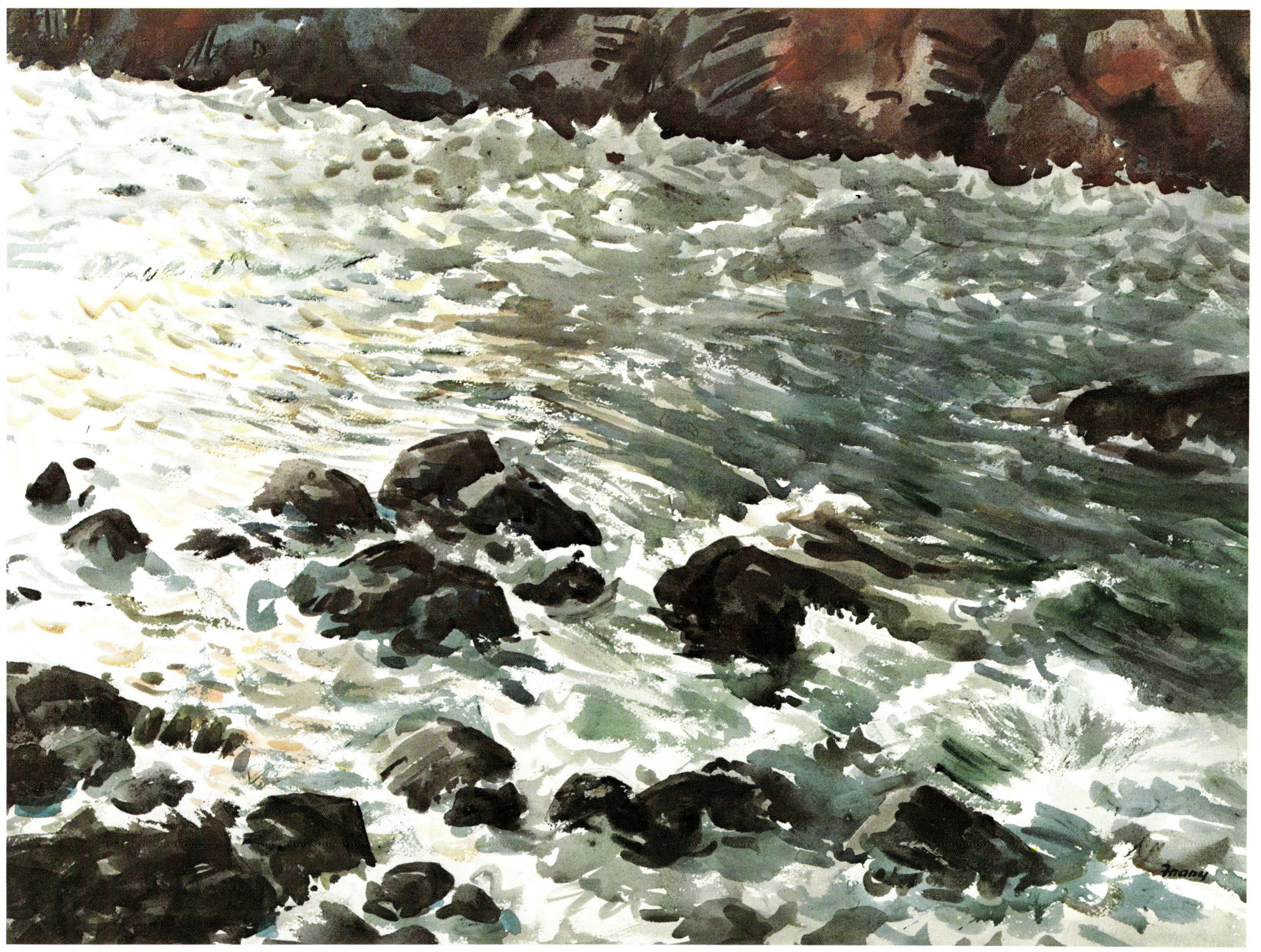

41. *Lunch Break near Burro Bluff Rapids*

We reached this spot about halfway through the Lower Canyons on the third or fourth day out. This is one of the most inaccessible places in the United States, truly *despoblado* ("unpopulated"). There are only a few primitive access roads. In an emergency, it is necessary to go the full distance before leaving for Dryden, a gas station–store twenty miles north.

We had open canoes. Each canoe carried two duffle bags containing the bedroll and personal gear of each passenger. Besides that, every canoe had its share of tents, cooking equipment, and supplies and carried a five-gallon jug of water, life jackets, and extra paddles. I also had my water-color equipment. Full sheets of 22″ x 30″ watercolor paper do not fit well in canoes, and I often felt that my painting material was almost the "straw that broke the camel's back." My equipment was tied down in plastic sacks, and everything stayed fairly dry. My fellow travelers were good sports, so everyone had pleasant, memorable experiences.

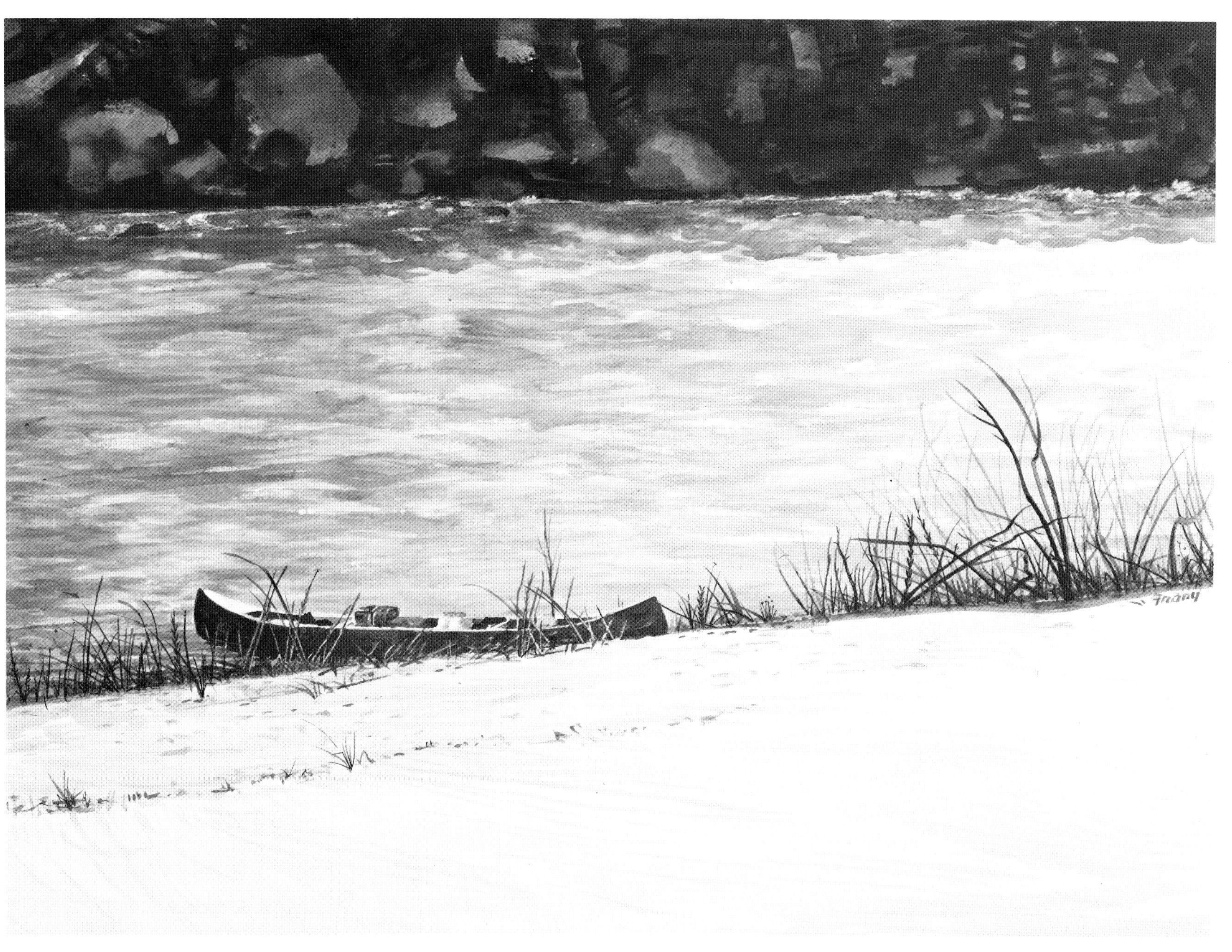

42. Near San Ygnacio

I "discovered" San Ygnacio, a sleepy little village thirty-three miles south of Laredo, on the bank of the river. It has many fine architectural details. This is near Falcon Dam, which backs up some three million acre-feet of water to make this reservoir the largest on the river. I saw many varieties of birds here.

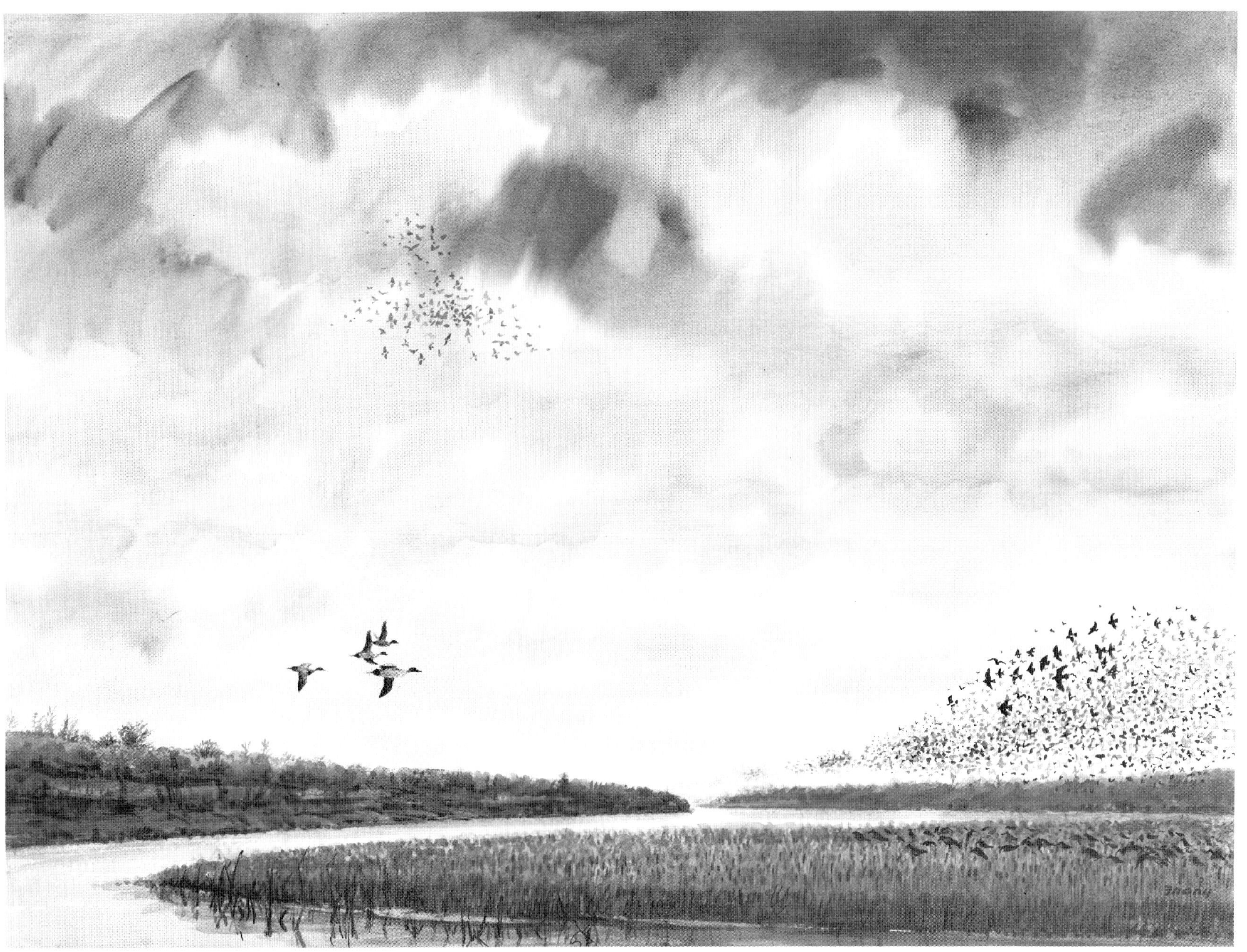

43. Church at Camargo, Mexico

This clean little Mexican town seems to be in contrast to Rio Grande City, across the bridge on the U.S. side of the river. Rio Grande City has a notorious reputation for smuggling and other illegal border-related activities. A resident of the town said in defense, "Our reputation is not true. We trust each other—we leave our guns in our unlocked pickups, and nobody steals anything." While I was painting this, a young man was touching up the spills of another young fellow, who was painting the red trim on the belfry.

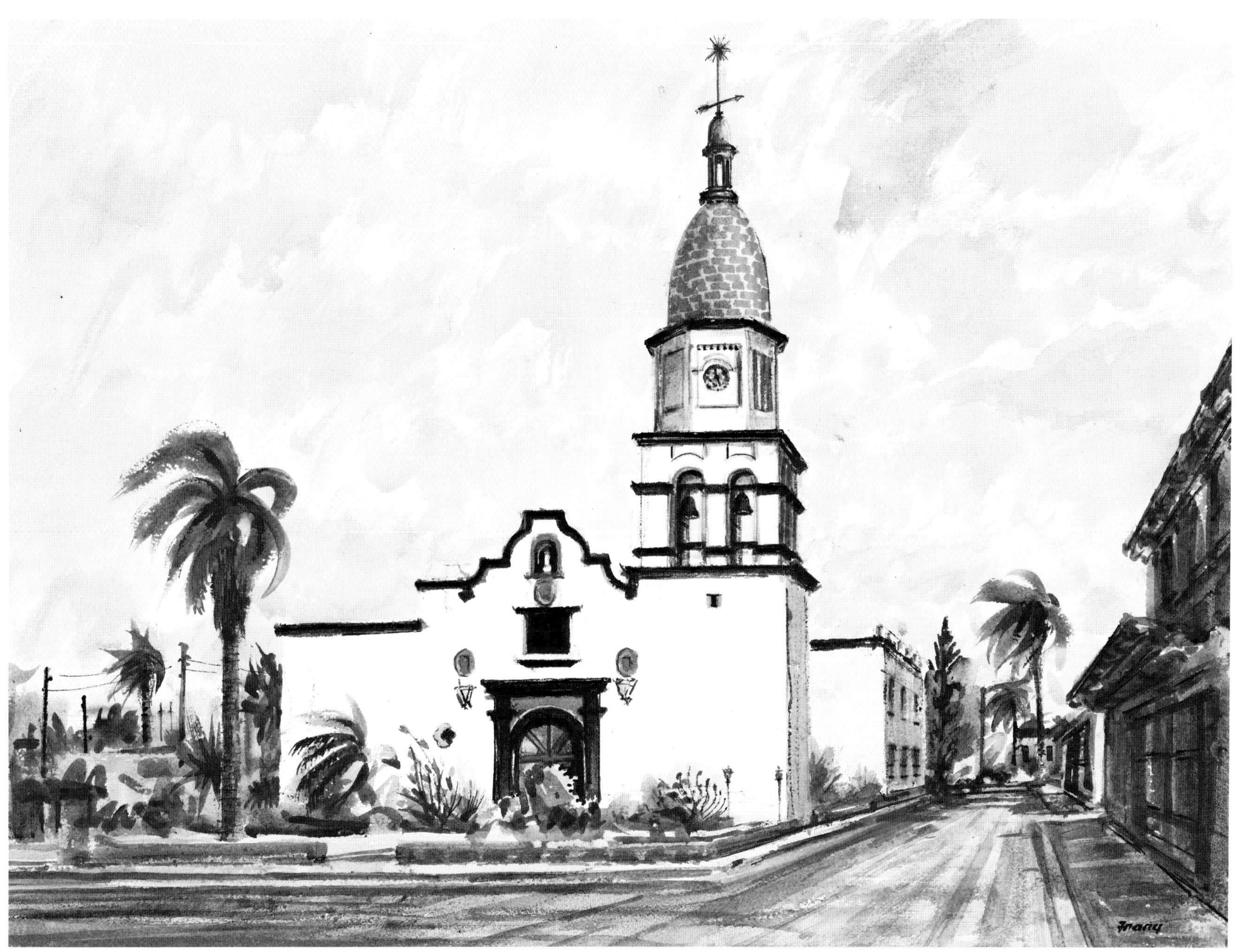

44. Hand-Pulled Ferry at Los Ebanos

There are many small border crossings from Falcon Lake to the Gulf of Mexico, but one of the most unusual is Los Ebanos ("the ebonies"). This is the only hand-operated ferry on the U.S. border. It is an experience to have your car pulled across the Rio Grande by these four jovial operators. The fare is minimal and is even less coming back.

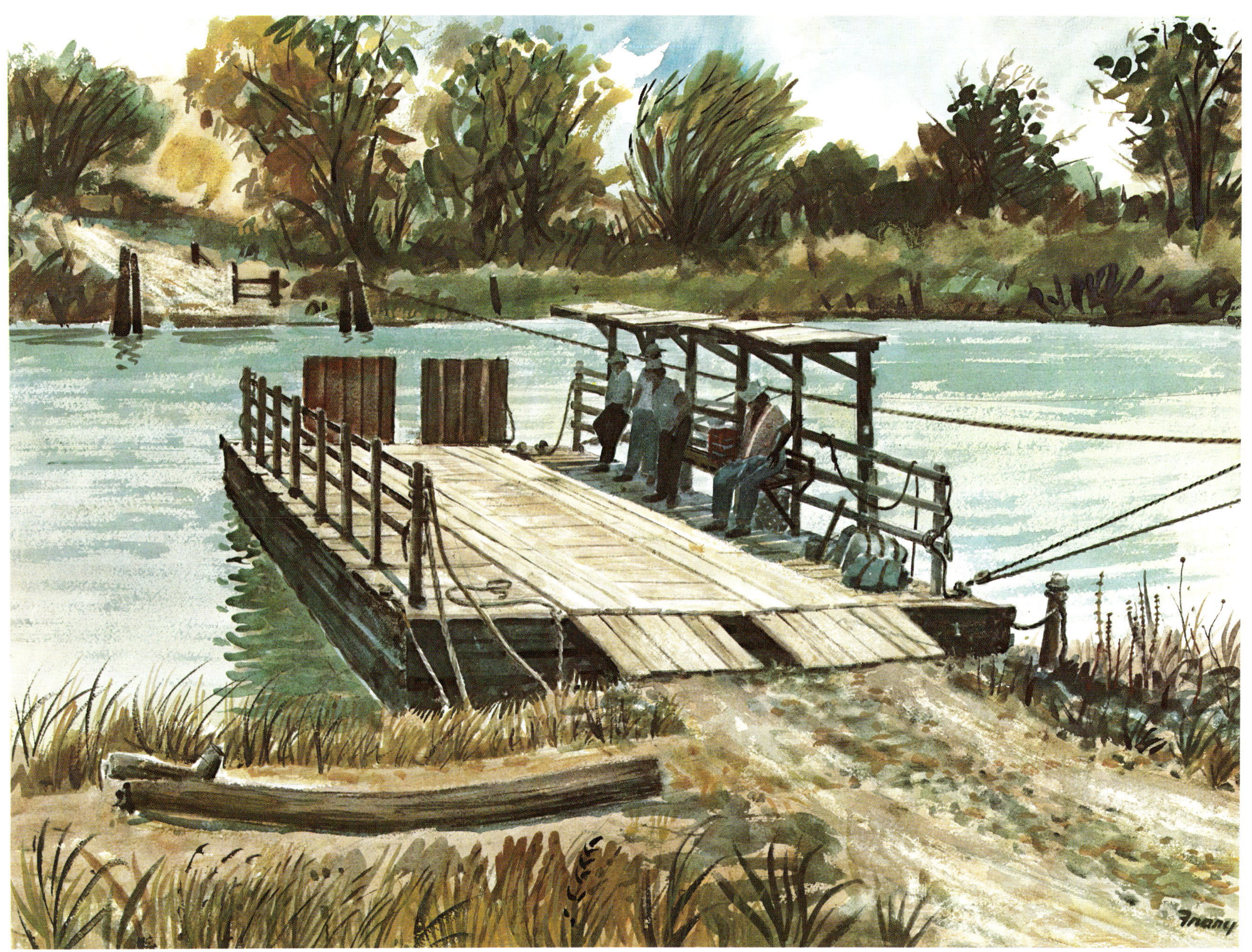

45. Los Ebanos Border Station

About a mile into Mexico from this border crossing is the small, nontourist town of Diaz Ordaz. When I recrossed the border I found the customs official to be very efficient: he confiscated a grapefruit that I had brought into Mexico two hours before.

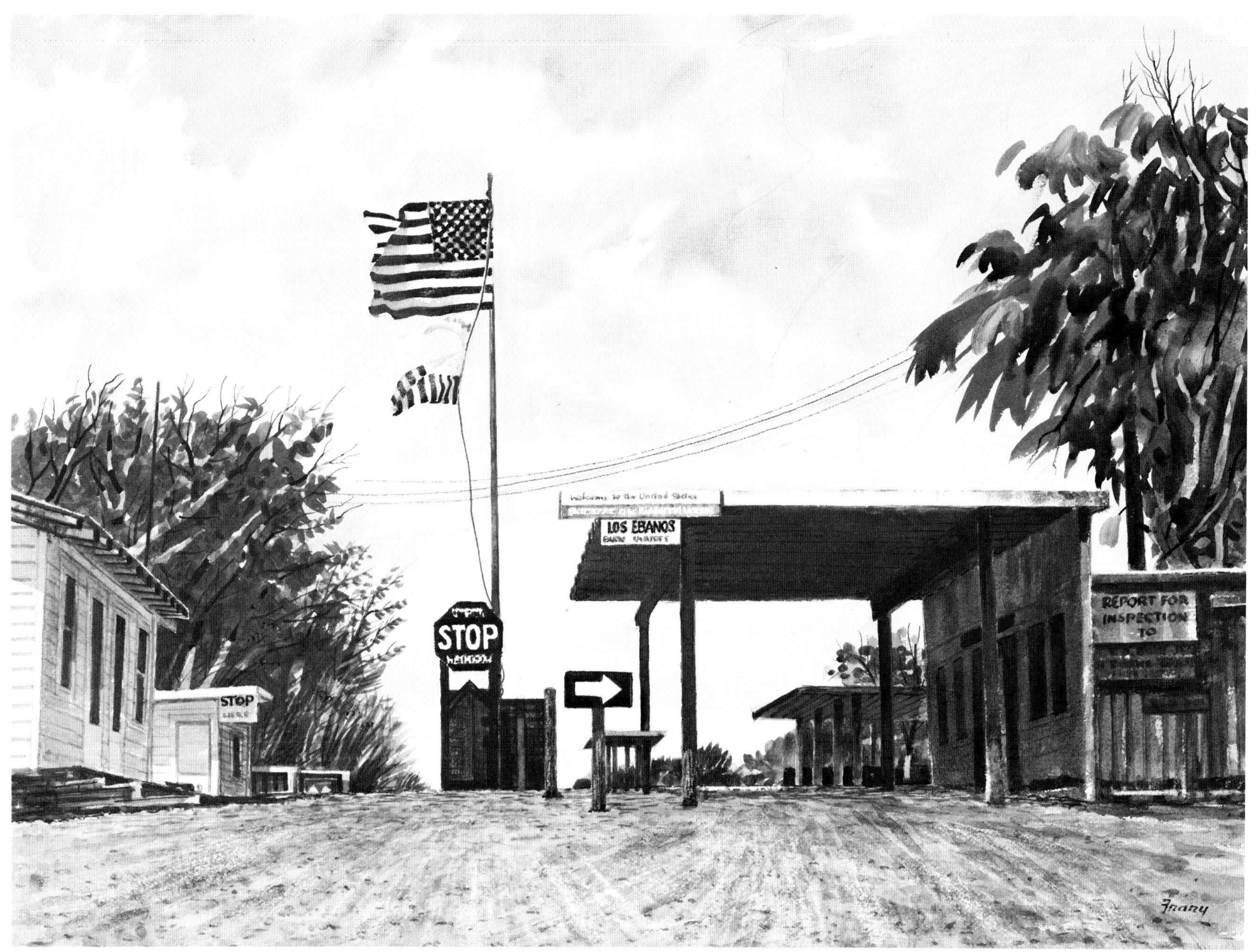
Welcome to the United States
LOS EBANOS
STOP
STOP
REPORT FOR
INSPECTION
TO
Franz

46. The Fertile Rio Grande Valley

From Rio Grande City and Mission east is one of the most agriculturally productive areas anywhere. The flat, alluvial plain lends itself to irrigation, and the tropical climate plus the water of the Rio Grande make possible a huge production. The climate, which attracts tourists and retirees from the north, keeps the population of the Rio Grande Valley growing at a steady rate.

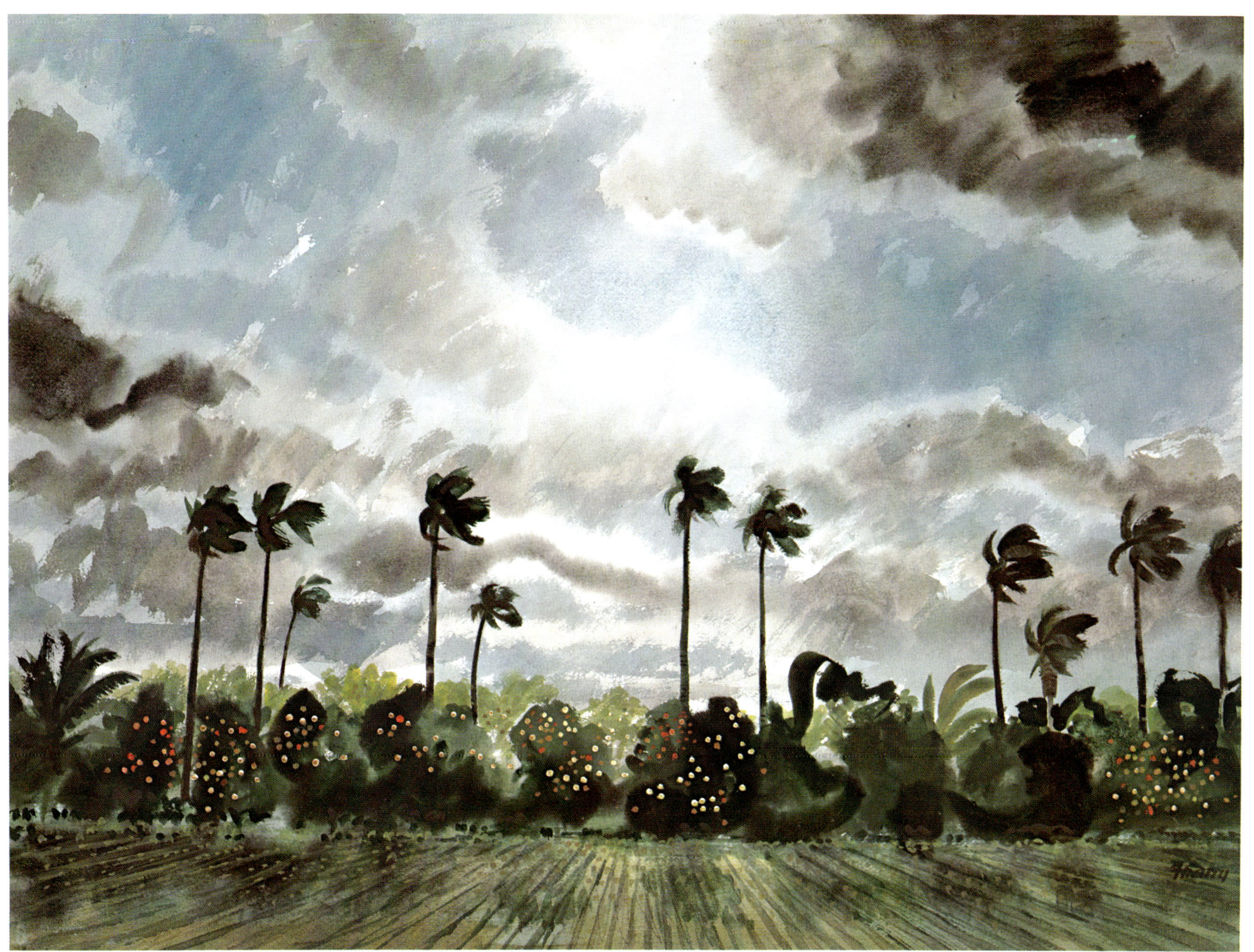

47. Boca Chica

The Rio Grande meanders and curves back on itself through the last of its voyage to the sea. It is not unusual to be in South most, near Brownsville, and look north across the river, into Mexico. Finally, the Great River flows out strong and surprisingly clear into the Gulf of Mexico at lonely Boca Chica ("little mouth"). I was disappointed that there are no buildings, markers, or monuments to signify the end of the great journey.

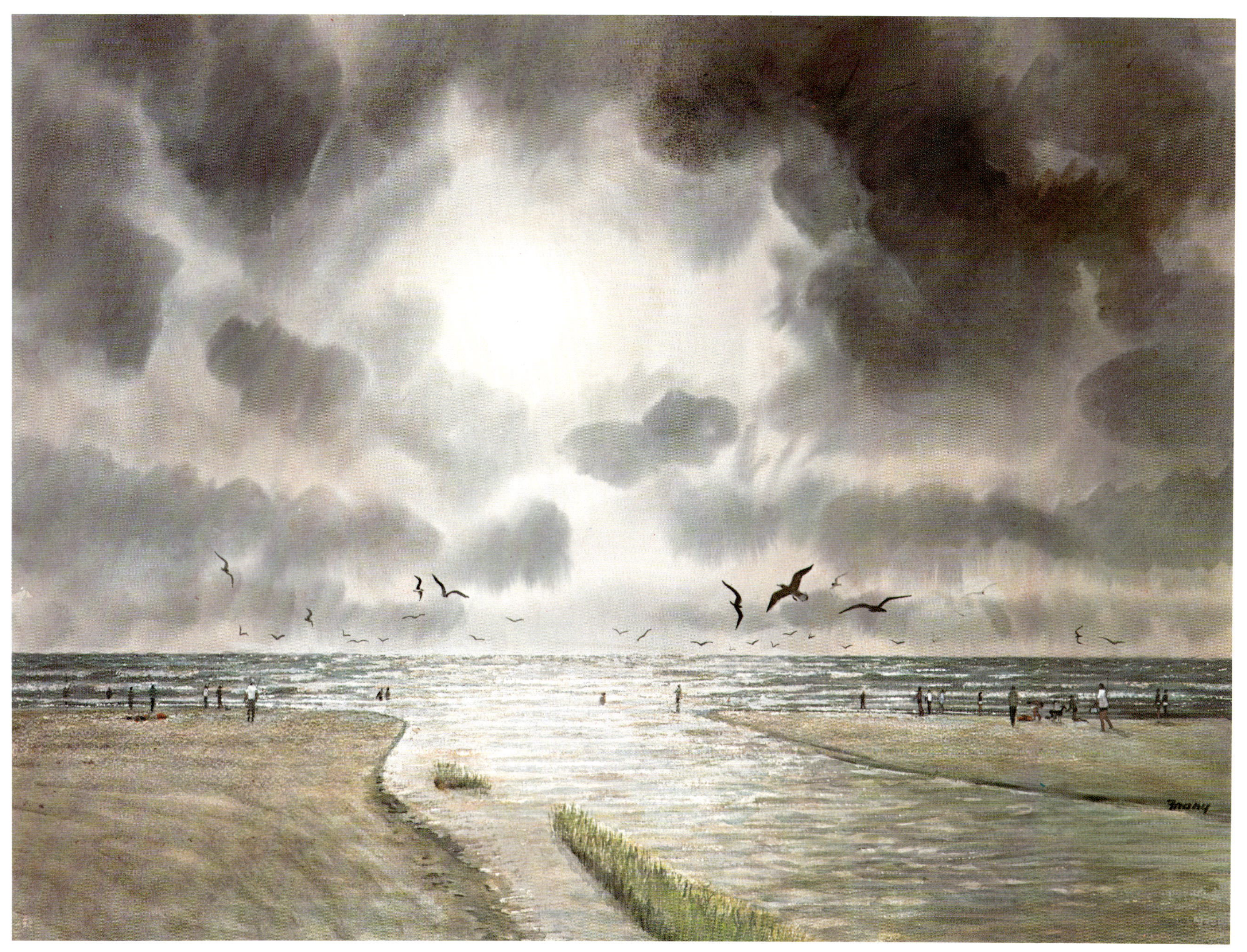

48. Sunrise on the Gulf

As the Rio Grande flows into the Gulf of Mexico toward the rising sun, it is perhaps a symbol that it is not the end of a great river but the beginning of a new cycle—another change in our wondrous planet.

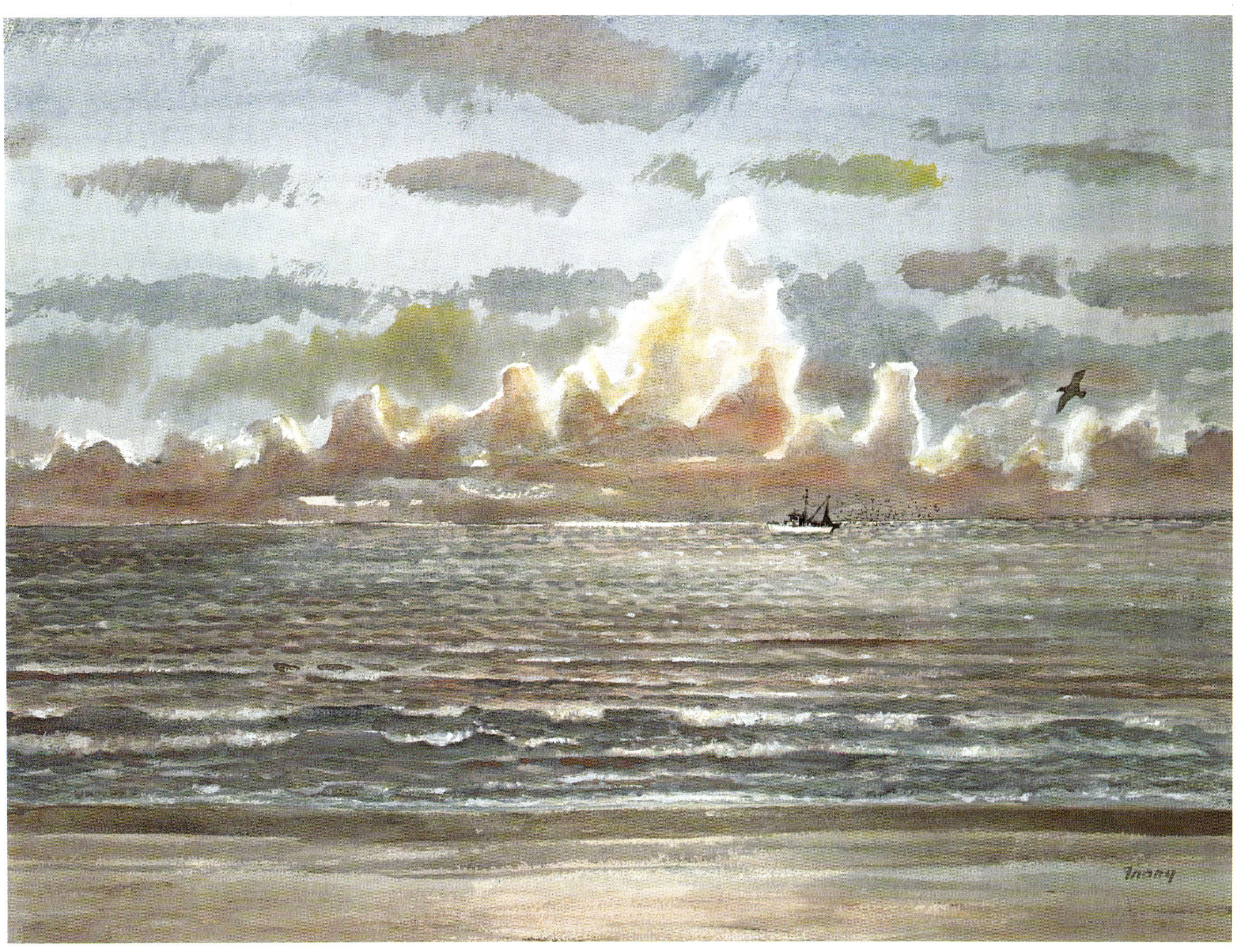